Page One Publishing Private Limited
20 Kaki Bukit View
Kaki Bukit Techpark II
Singapore 415956
Tel: (65) 6742-2088
Fax: (65) 6744-2088
enquiries@pageonegroup.com
www.pageonegroup.com

Produced by
Page One Publishing Private Limited

Editorial Director
Kelley Cheng

Editor
Serena Narain

Authors
Tatjana Johnsson & Marión Bravo-Bhasin

Photographers
Edward Hendricks and Alan Lee

Designer
Frédéric Snauwaert

Printed and bound in China

in style asia
copyright © 2008 page one publishing private limited

First published in Europe 2008 by:
Links International
Jonqueres, 10, 1-5
08003 Barcelona, España
Tel: +34 93 301 21 99
Fax: +34 93 301 00 21
E-mail: info@linksbooks.net
www.linksbooks.net

Distributed by:
Links International
Jonqueres, 10, 1-5
08003 Barcelona, España
Tel: +34 93 301 21 99
Fax: +34 93 301 00 21

IN STYLE ASIA

By Tatjana Schantz Johnsson
Words by Marión Bravo-Bhasin
Photography by Alan Lee
& Edward Hendricks

Contents

Foreword

In today's ever expanding global world, we are all probably decorating and furnishing our homes with some degree of Asian style. Its far-reaching influence has had a major impact on Western style since the days of Marco Polo. From Chinoiserie to fine porcelain, chintz prints, Zen style, Bali style, Indian glitz and batiks, it's impossible to not fall in love with Asia's colours, textiles, light, form and aesthetics. After living in Asia for six years, I certainly have.

For me, Asia is all about a painter's palette of colours, and an almost palpable ancient mystique and aura. The cheerful, sometimes somber but never boring colour combinations never cease to inspire me. The hot, humid climate along the equator; the colourful local garments; the ornate temples and shrines all bring some element of wonder to daily life. Asia is exotic and intoxicatingly fascinating. Trying to capture some of that exotic charm is what I am after – capturing it and bringing it into your home and life. One of the reasons for Asian style's appeal and longevity in the decorating world is that it blends beautifully with all styles, from modern to rustic and everywhere in between. It will look good no matter if you live in a large western urban city or in a breezy dwelling on a Thai beach.

Surround yourself with the colours you love and with furnishings that speak to your senses. Experiment with arranging and displaying your collections, travel mementos and favourite items in original, unexpected ways. Mix not only Eastern and Western items but old and new, classic with a little sprinkling of kitsch. Listen to your instincts and let them guide you in creating a personalised home. An eclectic mix is so much more interesting and welcoming than one static look from wall to wall.

For all of us who appreciate the exotic beauty of Asia and the multitude of palettes and combinations that coexist so effortlessly, this book is for you. Decorating Asia takes you around the region to eleven varied, complex and diverse countries presented in a completely contemporary manner, inspired by the mood and vibe of the land and its people. It's not about doing up your entire home to resemble a traditional Thai or Japanese or Indian home. It's more subtle, whimsical and unexpected. It's inspirational.

The following pages are my look into Asia and what colours, shapes and materials inspire me from these fascinating lands. And since, sometimes a picture does not always tell the entire story, the text is aimed to add to the reader's appreciation and insight into the culture and to help explain the why and where things, customs and colour preferences originated from. The recurring themes, complex histories, co-mingling of religions and native beliefs in these countries only add to the Eastern mystique. From the sunny, tropical shores of the Philippines to the rugged, vast steppes of Mongolia, Asia is sure to speak to one on various levels. May you soak in the beauty, unveil the inspiration and be motivated to bring Asian accents into your home.

Tatjana

China

Ancient and Modern

"Chinese style is timeless and universal. Prints, lanterns, furniture, it all looks amazing in old, Chinese homes and in new, western homes. I don't really know why – the design, the details, their intrinsic harmony and balance – but I don't get tired of appreciating them." – Shihong, musician.

After all these years, China still intrigues. With a civilisation dating back over 4,000 years, fascinating dynasties, complex history and a hugely influential artistic aesthetic – China seems new again. Chinese style is evident throughout the world, from red lantern-filled, Qing style Chinese restaurants to sleek and simple Ming dynasty chairs found in homes from Buenos Aires to Shanghai. Great design endures and today, from ancient China to modern China, it still looks good.

Since the time the first European explorers travelled to Cathay (as China was known in the Middle Ages) and began to return with porcelain, silk, lacquer and ivory, the West has been besotted with all things Chinese. So much so was the European demand for exotic items from the East that an entire style – Chinoiserie – was born to keep up with the demand. Chinoiserie originated as European-made alternatives, not reproductions; to the Chinese artefacts e.g. European-made pottery and porcelain with Ming style designs, Italian embroidery with Chinese symbols and motifs. The Chinoiserie movement eventually grew to encompass not only porcelain, textiles and furniture but also home interiors, fashion, gardens and architecture.

How to begin to define or interpret Chinese decorating style? Like style of any kind, it's completely dynamic and individual. But undeniably, if you are after a Chinese "look", there is no going wrong if you start with red. China is red; fire-cracker red, cinnabar red, oxblood red and pure red. For the Chinese, red is deeply, culturally linked. Even before the Manchu rulers of the Qing Dynasty brought a more intense, lavish use of colours and décor, red was already strongly embedded in the culture as a symbol of happi-

ness. Red symbolises luck, joy, passion, justice, triumph, prosperity, blood as a life force – in a good way – and fire and energy. There is no stronger symbol than a pair of red doors to bring luck into one's home. Or the traditional, red-swathed matrimonial bed; or the auspiciously red *hong bao* packets used to present money and good wishes at weddings, birthdays and special holidays. Or the red lantern; or the red-dyed eggs presented to guests at a baby's one month birthday; or vermilion red palatial walls.

If China is red, then it's also black. Ink black. Stone black. The colour combination is classic, stylish and still so modern – the *yin* and the *yang*. Black symbolises *yin*, or the female along with water, moon, winter and rejuvenation. Conversely, red is representative of the male; *yang*, and symbolises fire, sun, summer and activity. If you are after a timeless elegance, it's hard to beat a lustrous black enhanced by a deep sumptuous red. Just think of all the beautiful Chinese black and red lacquerware boxes. Over 7,000 years ago, the Chinese started making lacquer pieces in traditional black and red colours and since that time, black lacquer has always been considered mysterious, sophisticated and stylish. Of course, great style doesn't end with colour and when you are after a Chinese look, there is a wealth of inspiration from propaganda style statues and posters to delicate pastoral scenes on wallpaper. The Chairman Mao image, the graceful strokes of calligraphy and the carved, detailed and symbolic designs on metal locks, textiles, ceramics, stones, artefacts and so much more. It's become increasingly easier and more inexpensive to indulge in all things gentle and Chinese inspired – exotic embroidery, rich brocades, blossoms and bird motifs.

During the Cultural Revolution, Mao's image hung in every home, classroom, office and public building. People showed their loyalty by wearing his face on a badge, by emulating the way he dressed and by honouring him – drawing his image on mirrors, clocks, and other paraphernalia. Today, his ubiquitous image brings an element of eclecticism to contemporary interiors.

Lucky dragon. The dragon is one of the most auspicious and sacred of Chinese images. Dancing dragons symbolise bravery, power and nobility. Here they adorn a carved lacquer box.

2

3

Chinese calligraphy is discipline and art in a brush stroke. It takes pure discipline to control the brush, hold it properly and restrain oneself so the movement of the brush on the paper is precise. And it's as individual as the artist. For the Chinese, the brush-work is a direct expression of the artist's personality. When asked to describe Chinese sensibilities and style, China-born architect Calvin Tsao remarks that the double happiness characters embody the sensibilities, "It can be both pattern and word. The style and the aesthetics are embodied in meaning". One could apply that same thought to Chinese calligraphy.

Chinese decorative details speak volumes. Throughout its history, Chinese emperors were the style arbiters and keepers of artists and craftsmen that produced work of exquisite workmanship. Skilled craftsmen transformed the mundane and common into works of art – boxes, cups, utensils, baskets. Every aspect of creating something was carefully considered. In furniture for instance, the metal-ware was not only seen as functional but also decorative. Made from brass or other alloys, hinges, handles and locks were considered of major significance to the overall design and often include intricate carvings. Themes and motifs ranged from nature to symbols of virtue, luck and prosperity. It's common knowledge that the Chinese people are extremely superstitious and firm believers in the power of colours, numbers, animal and nature symbols. This fascinating aspect of Chinese design adds an entirely new dimension and appreciation to the items – just as every stroke completes the character, every design tells a story.

1   The generous curves and ample depth on this rattan and black lacquer opium bed call for lounging and a little mystery.
2   Detail on a bronze ding vessel.
3   Intricately carved doorways and pillars line the entrance to the temple courtyard.

1

2

1   Close up of a temple painting.
2   An opium pipe stowed away in a decorative case.
3   Burning temple lights.
4   A wooden tea tray serves as the perfect frame for a collection of Chinese curios from a bone eyeglass case (far right), brass seals, ceramic tea cups to a bone pillow.

1   An antique war strategy book is bound with intricate detail.
2   Stroke of genius. A hanging collection of calligraphy brushes adds an instant Eastern outlook to a work studio window.
3   The large calligraphy love poem and Asian-influenced coffee-table add the China touch to this modern seating area.

大江東去浪淘盡千古
風流人物故壘西邊人
道是三國周郎赤壁亂
石穿空驚濤拍岸捲起
千堆雪江山如畫一時多
少豪傑遙想公瑾當年
小喬初嫁了雄姿英發羽
扇綸巾談笑間檣櫓灰飛
煙滅故國神遊多情應笑
我早生華髮人生如夢一
樽還酹江月 蘇東坡
念奴嬌赤壁懷古
丙寅新夏羅叔重書

1   *The art of display. Antique trunks, a Buddha statue, lantern and calligraphy scroll stack up nicely because of their common colour tone.*

2   *A Chinese character detail on a red porcelain bowl.*

3   *A velvety, soft red rose is a subtle way to offset some of the hardness of the table's sharp edges and lines.*

4   *Asian simplicity. A square, crimson lacquered table elegantly set with red and black lacquerware. The table's generous space
even allows for a bronze reproduction of Jane Poupelet's Woman Bathing to occupy some space and infuse some quirky fun.
The straight lines of the couplet signboards and the wedding cabinet set against clean white walls keep the feel contemporary.*

1

1   The Chinoiserie touch. Detail of a contemporary Ming toile printed cloth.
2   Vintage-looking Asian packaging from talcum powder to almond cookies has always captured the western interest.
     Alongside some heirloom silver pieces, the feel is completely soft and feminine, and perfect for a powder room.
3   A perfectly proportioned red and black detailed, cast iron bathtub.
4   The Shanghai Girl hasn't lost her appeal. Calendar girl pin-up posters were popular in the 1920s and '30s
     to sell everything from cigarettes to soap. Today their romantic appeal is still admired.

2

3

4

1

2

Chinese style and influence is all around us today and remarkably it is practically impossible to not be enthralled, influenced and inspired by its diversity and simplicity. In fact, it is almost impossible to not own something that hasn't already been touched by its far-reaching appeal. From the plum blossoms on your cushions, to the glorious blue and white design on your porcelain plates, China style is here to stay. As the following pages show, it's increasingly easy to incorporate Chinese elements to any contemporary home but more importantly, it's when the elements are mixed with other eras, or modern furniture or unexpected surroundings that their inherent charm is truly exposed. Chinese style – use it sparingly or lavishly, but enjoy it.

1   *Simplicity, balance and colour instantly ooze the Chinese aesthetic in this bedroom.*
2   *A deep red anthurium in an organic-shaped vase plays up the sculptural qualities of both, while the colour combination adds pure drama. The red coral candleholder in the background adds height and interest to the arrangement.*
3   *A Chinese Dragon Opera robe makes an ideal wall hanging with its simple, architectural design, while the heavy gold embroidery offsets the clean lines of the black lacquer desk and yoke-back chair.*

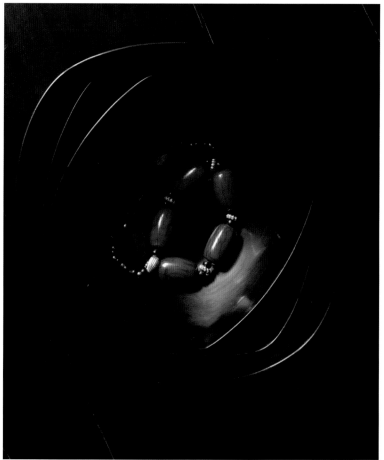

1 A trio of soup spoons and matching bowls on a mat of fresh, lucky bamboo.
2 Simple beauty, three black bowls and a coral necklace.
3 Decorative motifs. Brightly hued wedding cabinets with auspiciously detailed metal hardware are designed to bring good luck to the married couple.
4 Chinese medicine cabinets are generally lower and wider than a standard cabinet, and are standout pieces on their own with their numerous pull-out drawers and painted Chinese characters.

1   Street scene in China.
2   Below, Mao Zedong's far-reaching influence is still apparent, especially in the older generation who lived during the Cultural Revolution.
3   Two iconic and wildly popular Chinese images in home decorating today – a lantern and a kitschy porcelain statue of a saluting Chairman Mao Zedong.
4   Ancient, modern, glorious China inspiration.

Singapore

Multi-cultural and Cosmopolitan

"Since the overwhelming majority of the population lives in small, high-storey housing complexes I think the local style is more simple and functional than highly ornate and fussy. But there is a definite move towards creating a more personalised space with various ethnic influences, not just drawing from one's own heritage." – Siew Fun, graphic designer.

Singapore is a unique country in Asia. Unique for many reasons; first, it is a young nation, having declared its independence from Malaysia only in 1965; secondly, its paternalistic, unflinching government-style has lead it to remarkable growth and success in such a short span of time; and thirdly, the cultural mix of its Chinese, Malaysian and Indian people have retained their ethnic heritage while being heavily influenced by modern forces of the West. All of these factors, and more, have given Singapore its multi-cultural sensibility and its cosmopolitan edge.

From fishing village to thriving metropolis, Singapore today is tall skyscrapers, chrome slick architecture sitting next to decorative shophouses from the 19th and 20th century (so-called because their owners had shops in the ground level and resided in the upper level.) Located immediately below the tip of the Malaysian peninsula, and just a few degrees from the equator, Singapore is a fast-paced society with an Eastern face and a Western outlook. It's moving forward full-speed ahead, while trying hard to not let go of the values and traditions that have defined its past. It's a compact island of contrasts and diversity. It's the old and new, working together and looking great.

These two sides of Singapore, vying for attention and balance, are perpetually present and offer a collage of inspiration for home decoration. The rows of candy-coloured shophouses are a superb starting point. Emblematic of Singapore, the shophouse architecture and style has heavy influences from the nar-row-fronted houses of Amsterdam (with the strong presence of the Dutch colonist in Malaysia, Indonesia and the region, their influence was definitely profound in terms of architecture) and the courtyard houses of southern China. Multi-functional, low-rise (originally two stories although three- and even four-storey structures were subsequently built) and with ornate, coloured and tiled façades, the shophouses are a convergence of multi-ethnic influences. European neo-classical motifs such as the egg-and-dart mouldings and the Corinthian capitals on the decorative pilasters are commonly found on the structures as are Malay building traditions like the elaborate woodwork seen in the carved panels, louvres, screens and fretwork. From the Chinese, traditional mythological motifs like phoenixes were popular (symbolising that loyalty and honesty were in the people who lived there) and Peranakan pastel coloured glazed tiles, often with floral or geometric motifs are typical. The Peranakans, descendants of the early Chinese immigrant population of the Malay Archipelago are known for their richly detailed design, tiles, embroidery and beadwork.

The shophouses were commonly painted in pastel colours by the Chinese, Peranakans and Malays for they believed it brought good luck. Now, over 150 years on it is not uncommon to come across rows of renovated shophouses painted in modern, bold hues of orange, citrus yellows/greens and shades of vivid blue. Fortunately, as a result of the construction boom of the 1970s, the Singaporean government realised that a large part of their heritage was being demolished or ignored in the growing need for modernisation. By the 1980s, a major government conservation program was established and historic neighborhoods such as Chinatown, Kampong Gelam (Malay/Muslim Quarter) and Boat Quay (the city's original business and trading area along the Singapore River) were renovated and made relevant to today's society.

Photo collage "Enter Asia" by Singapore-based artist Ketna Patel magnificently captures the uniqueness and charm of local doorways.

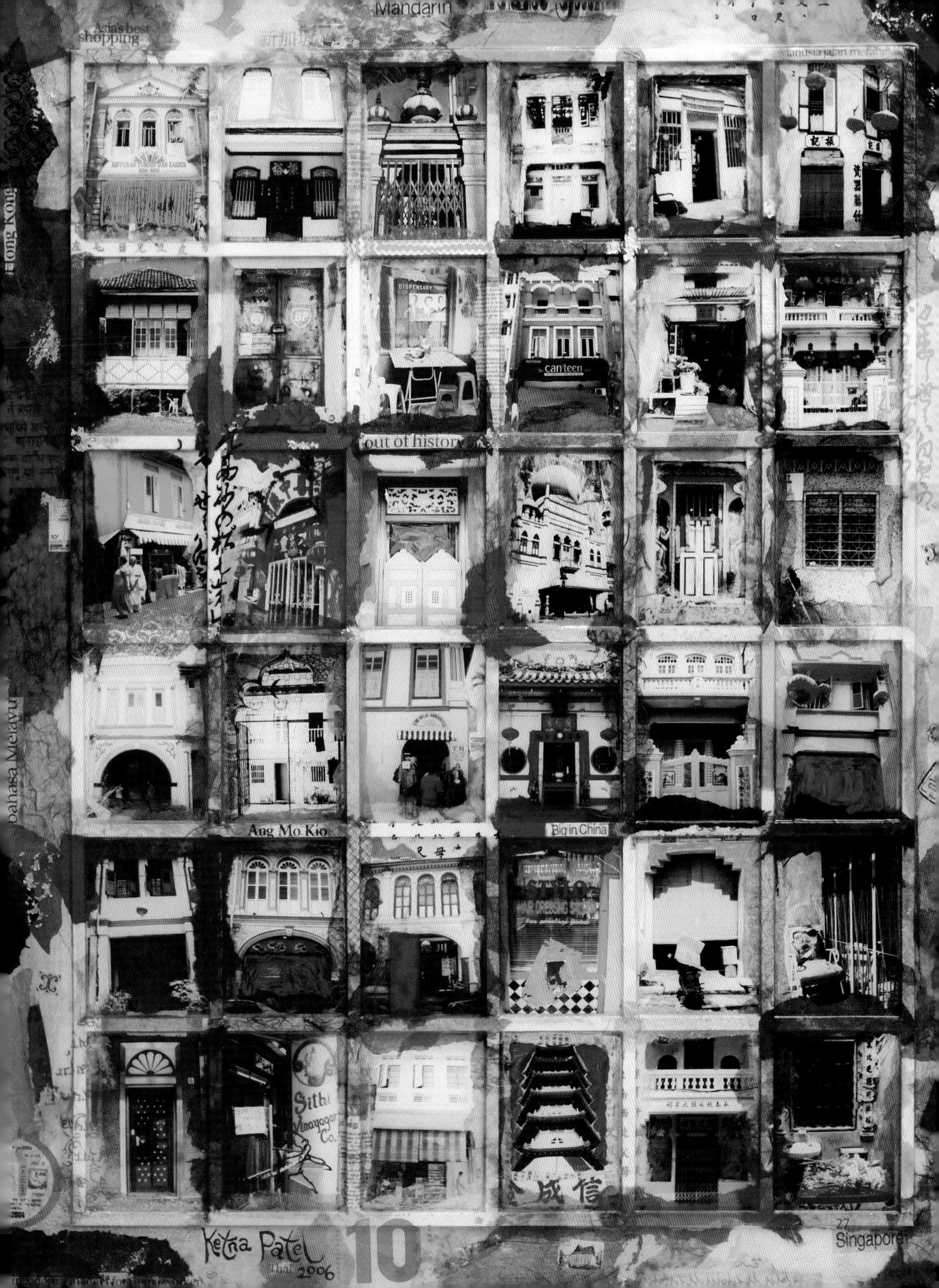

Asia's best shopping

Hong Kong

bahasa Melayu

out of history

DISPENSARY

can'teen

Ang Mo Kio

Big in China

Sithi Vinayagar Co.

Ketna Patel
Thai 2006

10

2004

1   Hand-painted mannequins by local artist Idrus Johor are as vivid and colourful as the Singaporean landscape.
2   Hindu temples dot the skyline alongside modern architecture and other places of worship.
3   Close-up of traditional shuttered shophouse windows.
4   Ornate, narrow and detailed are characteristics of Singapore's heritage shophouses.
5   Detail of ceramic, hand-painted tiles commonly found on the building façade.

And although the shophouses were originally white or pastel coloured, the modern bold coloured ones undeniable standout and look amazingly well-situated amidst the more somber surroundings. Yet, on the other hand, bright, vivid hues are a natural fit with the hot, tropical climate. Neon shades are apparent everywhere on this small island – from the signboards to the food, clothing and local flora and fauna. Transposing this vivacious colour palette into your home makes for an energy-filled, exotic space that exudes good cheer.

But it's not all about ethnic architecture and a kaleidoscope of colours. Glass, sharp-edged, chrome filled buildings are prevalent in the business districts and posh shopping centres. With construction practically a national pastime, it's a common joke that the construction crane is a popular skyscraper in the Singaporean landscape. Yes, new, improved, bigger buildings are the norm but it's also interesting to note that many of the new structures are still constructed with the thousand year old Chinese art of *feng shui*, or geomancy.

1   *Artist Ketna Patel's studio is a visual testament on how to live with art. Lampshades, lounges and artwork*
     are just a few of the vehicles she uses to display her vivid and eclectic collages of Asian life.
2   *Birdcages get a hip makeover with some neon paint and funky artwork. The oversized flip-flops (so emblematic of Asian life)*
     were made for an exhibition named Jalan Asia (Jalan means road in Malay).

previous spread

1 Simple, brightly hued shapes hold their own against the powerful artwork. Stairways and landings can offer some great display area for creative compositions – vases, a stool with Asian-flair and even a papier-mâché lion head and painted ostrich egg liven up the white space.

2 Would you like a paper towel? A little wit and art goes a long way in reinventing the common and everyday item such as this kitchen towel holder.

3 The Art Bridge by Pacita Abad enlivens the Singapore River along Robertson Quay. Philippine artist Abad was known for her use of rich colours, textures and shapes.

4 Despite the powerful surroundings of the side table, the vase and Buddha statue demand attention thanks to their standout texture and colour.

5 Art in a contemporary home can come in many forms, from paintings, funky statues and lamps to furniture. Be confident and choose what you love. A pop star Madonna-inspired lamp finds its home next to Mao, a collage and a barber's chair upholstered in Patel's pop prints.

1 A small sitting area in the library gets a splash of colour with the graphic tabletop and canary-yellow vase and chairs.

2 This magnificent snail shaped staircase found in a modern Singaporean home brings to mind the beauty of skyscrapers and awe-inspiring architecture.

1

2

Literally translated it means "wind water" and is the art of arranging the physical environment to harmonise with the nature of the individual or group. Doorways, walls and furniture must be properly aligned according to its principles to prevent good spirits, wealth and harmony from flowing out. Thankfully, bad *feng shui* can be corrected by using wind chimes, trigrams, mirrors or plants. Suntec City, the massive complex that opened in the 1990s is an excellent example of construction abiding by the principles of *feng shui*. The five towers stet are meant to symbolise the left hand with the world's largest fountain sitting in the palm of the hand, thus radiating wealth and prosperity (water is symbolic of life and wealth). Suntec City is Singapore's largest shopping complex and its success is largely attributed to its good *feng shui*.

1   *Vintage Chinese prints come into the 21st century with some confidence and guts. An enamel spittoon gets a new life as a flower pot and a small table is revived with a vivid floral "granny print" that has been decoupaged onto its surface.*
2   *Asian floral prints add immense charm to this already comfy reading area.*
3   *Mood boards are an excellent way to play, create and be inspired by what moves you. These arresting images beautifully capture the shades and tones of the shophouses and Singaporean life.*

1 Simple, straightforward lines and design evoke a contemporary aesthetic.
2&3 Modern Singapore skyscrapers reflect the new Asia.
4 A comfortable yet unconventional split-level loft room at the New Majestic Hotel. The hotel incorporates classic retro furniture with industrial details and quirky Asian art – the lightbulbs on the wall are artwork by local artist Justin Lee.

With so much change, construction and modernisation in Singaporean life, it is easy to understand why the people openly embrace all that is new. But when the old and new converge to create a unique, contemporary setting such as the New Majestic Hotel, nothing could be more inviting. This small, boutique hotel in Chinatown has a style all its own, combining clean design, classic furniture, personalised rooms by local artists and plenty of Asian influences in a revamped, conservation shophouse that really delivers the "wow "factor. Just another reminder that rooms do not have to be boring.

Colour always helps to tell the story, and for the modern Singapore look, it was natural to lean towards the red and white colour theme of the Singaporean flag. Not only does the flag symbolise pride and honour to its people, but also from a colour scheme point of view, it represents a pared down simplicity apparent in the "Singapore style." Red is not a surprising colour choice, given its auspicious association to the dominant Chinese population. While white, the confluence of all colours, is an appropriate pairing for it also could be said to symbolise the unity and harmony that is so important to Singaporeans.

1&2   Quaint, simple moments can still be found amidst cosmopolitan Singaporean life.
3   The sum is always greater than its parts. By clustering these simple, smooth vases next to the shapely lamp, a plain side table is transformed.
4   A sitting area from one of the rooms at the New Majestic Hotel. Singaporean artist Justin Lee's rendition of the flag is actually a montage of tropical flowers and the Chinese character "xi", which represents double happiness.

And of course, its modern, clean vibe is undeniable. If you are after a contemporary and visually striking feel, red and white is a classic way to go. Singapore may be small and young but it magnificently represents the new Asian aesthetic – an influx of cultural and religious influences, and a western appreciation of mod design, all while maintaining a distinct Asian flair.

1   *Skyscraper fun. This building block skyline makes for a playful centerpiece appropriate for a children's party or a colour themed tablesetting.*
2   *Seriously simple, yet stylish dining. If you're lucky enough to have a fabulous view, be sure to make the most of it with plenty of glass and windows. The smooth, modern lacquer table plays up Asian simplicity and the natural beauty of the bamboo plant in the background.*
3   *City slicker kitchen. A glossy white, black and red kitchen mirrors the new Singapore – industrial, functional and practical. The sharp and linear surfaces make for a clean and contemporary work area.*

1   *All wired up. Give your home a touch of industrial, futuristic chic with steel, Lucite, chrome and woven wire. The clear table, wire open-back chair and ethereal lamp all complement each other because of their see-through and architectural-like qualities.*

2&3   *Close-up shot of the Esplanade – Theatres on the Bay, the striking performing arts centre that was completed in 2002. Spiky sunshaded devices cover the two domes and are often likened to two durians – the large, spiky fruit that is a local favourite.*

4   *Lee's tribute to the extraordinary Samsui Woman who helped build Singapore. Samsui (literally mountain and water) women were a special breed of women from the Samsui districts of the Kwang-tung province of China. Bred with a physical and emotional strength unique to Chinese women, and fleeing China to escape marriage and gain independence, they worked alongside men in the same gruelling conditions of construction labour. Lee cheekily juxtaposes their image into a Mona Lisa pose and barrister's garment, symbolic of female endurance and the nation's lawful reputation. The red "hat" is also emblematic of the characteristic Samsui headwear.*

India

Harmonious and Flamboyant

"India is about excess and harmony – over a billion people, disorderly traffic, blaring music and horns, a kaleidoscope of colours, a patchwork of patterns. A recipe for chaos, for sure, but in the end, it works, it moves ahead and it coexists harmoniously. It's unpredictable and exciting. It stirs the senses." *– Arjun, costume designer.*

If you're looking for a treasure chest of decorating ideas, look no further than India. Its anything goes attitude, uninhibited use of colour, artistic knack for decorating anything and overall creative spirit makes it a feast for the senses and soul. From textiles, intricate patterns, architecture, temples and embellished and elaborated everything – India is inspiration incarnated.

The diversity within the sub-continent is varied and extreme. The geography; the Moghul, Portuguese, Dutch, French and British colonial influences; the Hindu, Islamic, Buddhist, Christian, Sikh, Zoroastrian and Jain religions; diverse and complex cuisines; 16 official Indian languages and over 1,600 dialects and let's not forget the sheer size of this nation of over one billion people, and generalisations become hindered. It's been said of India that anything you say about the country and its people – the opposite is also true. It's these extremes and truths that make India so endearing and memorable.

For many people, India connotes images of Rajasthan, the northern desert state known for its bright hues. Indeed, Rajasthan is justly famous for its glorious use of colour in the men's turbans,

the block print fabrics, special tie-dye techniques, the richly embroidered tribal desert shawls, mirrorworked blankets and the distinctly ornate northern *ghagra cholis* that the women wear (an embroidered, waist length blouse, full ankle-length skirt and veil or *dupatta* either draped across the neck or worn over the head). Amidst an arid and harsh natural environment, the use of colour naturally evolved as a means of survival (easily spotted in the landscape when wearing bright colours and mirrorwork) and a means to bring joy and comfort to life. The cities and villages have centuries old textile traditions and are known for their unique techniques, patterns, embroidery and colour combinations – at annual camel and cattle festivals it is possible to immediately deduce from a man's turban not only the district he is from but also his home village.

Colour is so closely associated with Rajasthani life that it comes as no surprise that entire cities are associated with a specific shade. Jaipur in Rajasthan is considered India's "Pink City" for the colour washed paint used to create the impression of red sandstone buildings of Mughal cities; Jodhpur is the "Blue City" for the blue painted houses that were either originally painted blue by the superior Brahmin caste to set them apart by rank and wealth or because of the blue pesticide paint that was used to stop ants and termites – stories differ but the colour is certainly popular today in many homes in Jodhpur; Jaisalmar is the "Golden City" named after the yellow sandstone used in all the house exteriors and that glow in the evening sun; and Udaipur is the famous "White City" for the beautiful marble palaces found along Lake Pichola.

A vintage hand-painted Bengali advertising poster retains the charm and style that is still so prevalent in Indian packaging, advertising and street graphics.

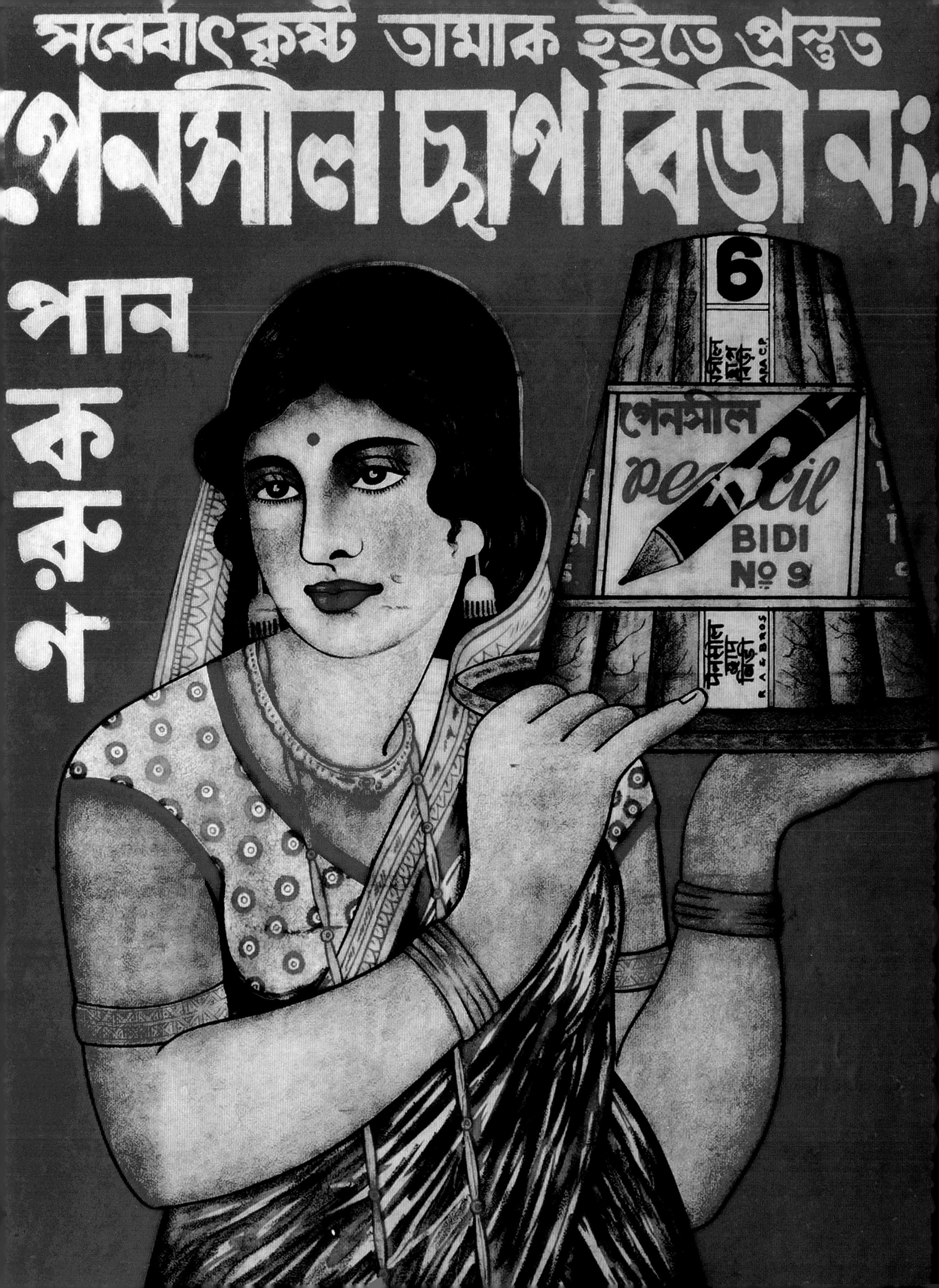
সর্ব্বোৎকৃষ্ট তামাক হইতে প্রস্তুত
পেনসীল ছাপ বিড়ী নং:
পান করুন
6
পেনসীল
BIDI
Nº 9

The north of India is also where invasions by Mongol, Turkish, Persian and Afghan Muslim warriors occurred and eventually led to over three centuries of Moghul rule. During this period (1526-1857), Indian artistic, intellectual and literary traditions evolved tremendously for the Moghuls had a fine taste, enjoyment and appreciation of cultural activities. They brought with them different styles of landscape gardening, cuisine, art and architecture that blended with the native Indian traditions to form a highly sophisticated style all of its own. The Muslim expertise in symmetry, abstract geometric and arabesque designs found a home in a land where animal and human forms dominated decorations made by the Hindus. The most famous monument existing today that represents the Muslim Moghul style is the Taj Mahal. Its breathtaking beauty not only lies in the impressively symmetrical gardens and monumental architecture but in the unimaginable detail, precision and skill used to decorate the entire structure, inside and out, with paint and stucco, stone inlay and carvings. Thankfully, there are still plenty of forts, palaces, intricately carved panelling, arches, domes, frescoes and other remains of opulent Moghul life. But of course, the bold use of colour, ornamentation and remarkable architecture is not just found in the North – it is innately Indian.

1 *Colourful Rajasthani puppets liven up the stone and muted architecture. Beloved stories from the Ramayana and Mahabharata epics continue to be crowd-pleasers and have helped the ancient craft of puppetry survive.*
2 *Rich detailing such as these gold threaded tassels with embroidered touches evoke sumptuous and ornate palace life.*

1   Food merchants excel in the art of display. The Hindu swastika symbol is commonly found as a decoration in food markets,
    houses, temples and in portraits of Hindu gods.
2   Colourful saris and jewellery are part of everyday life.
3   Plant beauty. The shape and colour of vegetables are nature's inspiration.
4   Men's turbans are not only worn for religious reasons but also to signify class, caste, profession or even a particular stage in one's life.
    Some turbans can be very elaborate to demonstrate wealth and power.
5   Moghul luxe. Soft velvet, deep tones and lots of embroidered details dress up this seating area and create a feast for the senses. The Middle-
    Eastern Muslim art form of embroidery, along with its precision with floral and geometric designs, was quickly adapted by the Moghuls of North India.

1 2

Colour and ornamentation is part of daily Indian life, there is no way around it. Colour is everywhere and plays a vital role in self-expression – from the exuberant saris and turbans, the hand painted mudguards on the rickshaws, the vibrant spice and food markets to the graphic film posters and billboards, adorned and painted horns on the cows, the ornate Hindu temples and even the painted faces of the holy men and Hindu icons. Think about it, what other country in the world would have a massive Spring Festival called *Holi* where colour is used to celebrate life itself? In a nationwide celebration, people take to the streets and throw fluorescent coloured powders (*gulal*) or water on everybody and anything.

The use of colour in India has many religious connotations, mostly related to Hinduism. For the Hindus, one of their principal deities worshipped is Agni, god of fire. All the colours of fire are symbolic for Hindus – red, orange and gold. The Hindus are married while sitting around a fire, and in death, they are cremated. Red is the traditional wedding colour for the bride's sari and during the ceremony a vermilion red bindi is placed on her forehead, along with red sindoor powder (made of zinc oxide) down the centre parting of the hair, to symbolise the woman's marital status. The bride's hands and feet are even intricately decorated with a dark red henna (*mehendi*) pattern that not only serves as another form of beautifying the bride but is also

1   *The harsh reality of village life is softened by the beauty and grace of the women in their splendid clothing.*
2   *A verdant hillside makes a beautiful backdrop to the ancient forts, temples and shrines that are to be found all over India.*
3   *Modern botanical prints make a spectacular wallpaper and create a striking contrast to the rustic and tribal feel of the loom needles.*

traditionally done for the cooling and calming qualities of the natural henna dye. Orange or saffron, as it is most often called in India, is also represented in the national flag. It's an extremely auspicious colour not only for the Hindus but also for the Sikhs, Jains and Buddhists. Lastly, gold or yellow are commonly found in India in the form of marigolds. These yellow flowers are typically used in their thousands in garlands and used as offerings for rites and rituals such as weddings, funerals and other ceremonies. Their potent yellow powers are such that during the festival of *Holi*, yellow water is often obtained by boiling water with marigold petals and leaving the liquid to soak overnight.

Blue is associated with the Hindu god Krishna, the embodiment of love and divine joy that destroys all pain and sins, and also the face of Hindu god Shiva, the destroyer but also the re-creator. In Hinduism, persons who have depth of character and capacity to fight evil are depicted with a turquoise, aqua blue skin. Blue is also symbolic of life itself as it represents water, the vast and vital seas and the cosmos, consequently the various shades have come to represent bravery, determination and ability to overcome difficulties. Blue exterior doors and archways can be found all over India. Today, blue is often used to paint the interior of homes for its cooling and refreshing properties.

Certain images instantly conjure exotic lands and India certainly has its icons, all closely associated with religion. For example Ganesha the Hindu deity of wisdom, prosperity and good fortune with the elephant head and human body; and the lotus flower, not only India's national flower but also deeply rooted to folklore and religious mythology. The unique manner in which the lotus grows – emerging from muddy waters, the long stalk rises above the surface into a glorious pink or white bloom untouched by the impurities below, lends itself beautifully to metaphor and symbolism.

1   Lotus blooms are combined with marigolds to make a thoroughly Indian floral arrangement. Indians are masters at decorating with flowers, from floor designs (rangoli), doorways, garlands and shrines – flowers are a vital part of daily life.
2   A glass mosaic artist at work.
3   A fine balance. Small, resin vessels matched with a few delicate flowers combine to make a visually appealing display.
4   This contemporary desert toned sitting area takes its lead from the sandy, orange and yellow shades of the Rajasthan scene depicted in the painting.

1

2

1   Within Jaipur's City Palace is the famous Peacock Gate. Painted stucco peacocks, India's national bird, surround the marble deity figurine and guard the entrance to the palace.
2   The blue painted houses in Jodpur rightly give the town its name, the "Blue City".
3   India hot and cold. The refreshing, cooling properties of the turquoise blue are a natural contrast to the spice and fire of chili red.

overleaf

A collage of Indian design, details and deities.

peace

Love

1

2

3

The lotus is both a divine symbol in Hinduism and Buddhism where it is represents purity in body, speech and mind. And of course, there is the sacred cow for the nation's Hindus and the national bird, the peacock often depicted in pictures with Indian gods and goddesses.

Alongside India's unmatched use of colour and religious symbols is the subcontinent's rich and ancient heritage of craft and artisan traditions. Richly influenced by the country's natural resources and the nation's large population (where techniques and ideas flourish), the art of hand-made goods and thousands of years of expertise are still to be found and not surprisingly, their appeal hasn't diminished at all. With the variety and uniqueness of Indian handicrafts, there is something to suit all tastes.

From the grandiose ancient temple cars of southern India to the most basic stone utensils, the craftsmanship of wood and stone masonry has evolved and pervades the entire subcontinent. Local tradition encourages homeowners to have a door frame of carved wood to welcome guests and balconies, window frames and beams are often made with brackets formed by carved animals, birds and human forms. This decorative style of work is commonplace in simple homes, palaces and temples. In contemporary homes, heavy, carved doors give an immediate feel of the exotic, while exuding warmth and protection.

Even metalwork with brass, bronze and iron, a tradition rich in creating useful, decorative and spiritually rich items has evolved and survived since early times. Brass water jugs are still used, as are copper vessels and beautifully carved metal *lassi* drinking cups from Moghul times. Utilitarian metal cups, trays and serving vessels have endured because of their clean, practical design and would still be at home in most modern homes. Also found, especially near temple sites, are the makers and sellers of bronze and brass figurines of the many Indian deities.

There are still many other forms of handicrafts such as pottery, papier-mâché, miniature paintings, leather and basketry to name just a few. But one art form deserves a special mention for it has been India's strength and unmatched forte since prehistoric times – textiles. Early leaders in the art of dyeing and patterning of cloth, the world continues to look to India for her textiles. Cotton and silk cloth, hand-woven in one of the many regional styles and most often embellished with embroidery, gold or silver threadwork, beads and even jewels, is integral to life in India. Thousands of years of expertise in block-printing, tie-dye, *ikat* and brocade weaving continue to produce exquisitely designed textiles of all kinds. Textiles serve as a true testament to the Indian craftsmen's ability to adapt their designs to suit various markets and trends, while combining their technical mastery in order to remain leaders.

1   *Two large, engraved brass water jugs are exemplary of the Indian expertise with metalwork and ornate detail.*
2   *A brass teapot, engraved tray and small decorative camel beautifully display India's folk art and craftsmanship.*
3   *The camel or "ship of the desert" makes a majestic image in the golden landscape of the northern Thar Desert.*
4   *Create an inviting sitting area with a plush chair and a unique background such as this Moghul-inspired room divider.*
      The miniature paintings and cut-out designs are reminiscent of palace windows and details, as are the decorative mirrors on the side table.

But how to put it all together in one's home? Certainly colour is the easiest way to go. Whether it's the desert hues of Rajasthan or the turquoise blues and pinks of the Hindu deities, a vibrant selection of tones adds energy to any home. Experiment with bold colour, pattern and texture combinations, cushion covers, sari fabrics and maybe a painted wall or two. Indian textiles in any fabric from silk, cotton to brocade are richly worked, regionally famous and impossible to not fall in love with. Invest in whatever your budget can afford and display it prominently – draped over a sofa, hung on the wall or stacked with other favourite pieces. A small icon placed on a mantelpiece, sideboard or table and intermixed with modern pieces will instantly stand out while seeming right at home. Look for rustic or tribal looking pieces or anything with a worn charm and the patina of age. It's the extra special layers of character and interest that you are after. A slightly uneven surface, distressed paint, it all adds to a beautiful imperfect finish full of charm and the human touch. This is India.

1   The unexpected and the beautiful live side by side in India.
2   Patterned wallpaper creates an instant Indian vibe and makes a wonderful starting point for some bold and fun decorating inspiration.
3   A small painted Ganesha statue finds a place at the base of a wooden offering stand.

1   Bollywood bench. A seating area pays tribute to Bollywood with graphic hand-painted posters, glitter, spangles and
     a lively arrangement of orange-toned cushions.
2   A cusped archway with impressive pattern and colour is matched by the heavy and solid brass door.
3   Lady fingers, a favourite Indian vegetable, make a beautiful display. Any fruit, vegetable or plant with a unique
     and striking colour or shape would make an inspired arrangement.

2

3

overleaf

1   Nowadays, ancient Indian practices have gone mainstream such as ayurvedic medicine, reiki and the many forms of yoga.
    These orange coasters with an ayurvedic roadmap to the body bring India and its mystical healing powers to the contemporary home.
2   Vivid graphics and neon colours impart some Bollywood panache to the statue.
3   From slippers to flowers, the exotic and beautiful has found a place in modern life.
4   Hand-dyed cloths and brightly coloured garments are everyday attire in India.
5   The Buddha Hand Citron is said to have originated in India and been brought to China by the Buddhist monks in the fourth century A.D.
    Fruits with "closed fingers" like these are said to be revered since it is believed to symbolise closed hands in the act of praying.
6   A coat armoire gets a mosaic-influenced makeover that combines effortlessly with a global mix of items, styles, patterns and colours.
7   Dressing up the entrance. Even a simple coat rack brings to mind Indian style with its display of vivid toned clothing and potpourri
    of interesting items below.
8   Indian textile workers are leaders in adapting to market needs. Traditional textile techniques such as this appliqué work quickly
    find its way onto wind-socks.

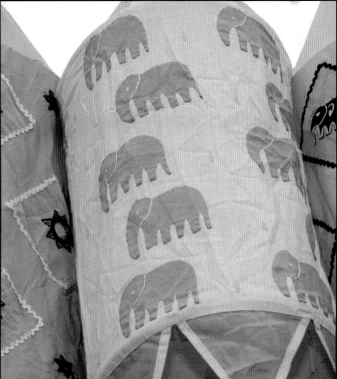

1   Jaipur, the "Pink City", is famous for its red sandstone buildings and impressive Moghul Palaces and Forts.
2   Nothing is left untouched. Painted water jugs and a painted wall show the love people have in India for decorating everything and anything.
3   Typical Rajasthani scene.
4   A large and rustic four poster bed gets a modern touch with a pair of metal arched floor lamps.

Cambodia, Laos and Vietnam

Spiritual and Serene

"More than a colour or combination of things, I see Vietnamese style a little like poetry – lyrical, graceful and sincere. Perhaps this is because material possessions tend to be few, so it's the blending of necessity with the spirituality and ancient soul of the land and people that defines Vietnam and even much of Southeast Asia." – Le Viet, advertising director.

Three distinct countries linked together by religion, customs, history and geography – Cambodia, Laos and Vietnam. Part of the Mainland Southeast Asian peninsula, these three nations, that constituted the former colonial French Indochina (1887-1954), also comprise a spiritual and serene beauty in its land and people not easily found in modern life. To visit one of these lands is to leave the 21st century behind and to step into a painting of welcoming people, fascinating cultures and stunning geography.

Cambodia, a nation of nearly 15 million people, is best known as the home to what is probably the largest religious building on earth, Angkor Wat. True to its name, Angkor meaning "city" or "capital" and Wat meaning "temple," this vast ancient architectural masterpiece is a great source of national pride (its image can be found on the country's flag) and of an increasing number of tourists each year. Built for King Suryavarman II in the early 12th century as his state temple and capital city, the temple is a showpiece of Khmer architecture. It was designed to represent Mount Meru, home of the gods in Hindu mythology, and later went from being a Hindu temple to a Buddhist temple. Much like the country's historical ties to India since the first millennium, Cambodia slowly moved from strong Indian practices and influences (primarily in law, religion, art, architecture, literature, language and writing) to the gradual shift to Buddhism mixing with its unique indigenous Khmer and other ethnic traditions. Today, 90 per cent of the population practices Theravada Buddhism.

Laos, a mountainous, landlocked country has been known to its people since ancient times as "land of the million elephants." With only around six million inhabitants and 70 per cent of the country consisting of mountains and plateus, Laos remains one of the last untouched places in Southeast Asia. Having only recently emerged from its war-torn history and turbulent past, the pace of life in Laos remains slow and relaxed thanks to its lack of outside influence. Enhancing the spiritual beauty of the country are nearly 5,000 Buddhist temples for the nearly four million practioners of Theravada Buddhism. Monks and temples colour the Laotian landscape. It is still expected today that every Laotian male become a monk for a short period of his life – usually between schooling and starting a career or getting married. Monks dressed in unmistakeable bright orange – the darker, more maroon colours are reserved for the wise, elderly monks – can be seen in the early morning hours collecting food and alms left by devout Buddhists, strolling peacefully through the city and even heard chanting in the temples. The colour of the monk's robes dates back to ancient times in India (the birthplace of Buddhism) when the philosophers would look into the forest and could always tell what leaves were about to fall because of their colour – yellow, orange or brown. Consequently, yellow became the colour of renunciation. To this day, Buddhist monks wear these colours as a reminder of the importance of not clinging, and of letting go.

If Cambodia and Laos represent the India in "Indochine," then most definitely the "Chine" or China refers to Vietnam. The Chinese have dominated Vietnam's history for over a millenium and their influence is far reaching with regards to Vietnam's political, literary, philosophical, military and religious beliefs. Although Buddhism is still the most practiced religion, it's a unique Vietnamese Buddhism that is intermingled with Confucianism and Taoism. Furthermore, Confucianism and Taoism as a religion and way of life are still very much in evidence today.

An altar life. The orange-coloured altar table lends itself beautifully for a unique display. A small lacquer stupa is used for offerings, as is the gold and orange joss paper on the wall. Next to the Asian stupa is a western crown that echoes the former's shape and form.

1

The largest of the Indochine nations, (population of over 85 million), Vietnam conjures images of the exotic, enchanting and the exciting. Rarely does someone return from a visit to Vietnam without admiration for its resilient and proud people; without a longing for its delicious food, baguettes and coffee; without a heavy dose of gratitude for having navigated successfully through the buzzing motorcycles and cyclos; and without a greater appreciation for human ingenuity and integrity. Vietnam's troubled past dominated the politics of the region since the mid-1900s. Starting with the anti-colonial struggle against the French, then a war between the new states of North and South Vietnam. In the late 1950s, the American government was drawn in and by the 1960s the fighting spilled across the neighbouring borders of Laos and Cambodia, submerging all in chaos, death and misery. It's been a slow but steady recovery for the region and Vietnam has grown the seed of tourism into a blossoming industry. The capital of Hanoi and the southern metropolis of Ho Chi Minh are bustling with lacquer vendors, galleries displaying prolific contemporary Vietnamese artists, and natural beauty and coastline to rival any neighbour.

1   Every morning the monks line up for their meal, prepared and given as alms by Buddhist followers.
2   Shades of saffron. The colour of the monk's robes dates back to ancient times in India when the philosophers would look to the trees and knew which leaves were about to fall because of their colour – yellow, orange or brown. To this day, monks wear these colours as a reminder of the importance of not clinging, and of letting go.
3   Orange toned simplicity. A modern tangerine covered sofa and similarly toned stools make an unfussy but inviting seating area.
4   Close up of the shapely prince Aha stool designed by Philippe Starck.

2

3

4

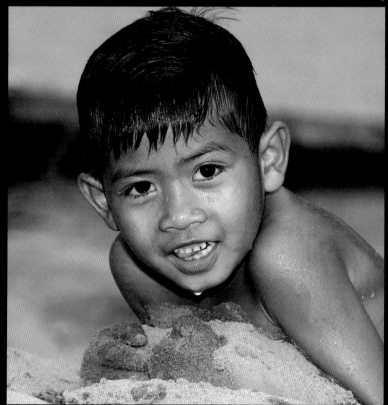

1

2

3

1 Serene simplicity. This teak dining area plays up its Asian charm with brightly-coloured silk cloths casually draped across the chairs, a simple floral arrangement and unfussy surroundings.
2 Angkor Wat temple complex.
3 The Khmer Buddha is known for its squarish-shaped head, large full mouth and rounded nose.
4 Khmer stone carvings from Angkor Wat.

1

2

1&2   Majestic colonial architecture from the 1930s such as the Victoria Angkor Resort and Spa is built in harmony with its
      environment and continue to evoke old world charm.
3   This light and airy contemporary living area also evokes old world charm with its large, dark furniture and Asian accents.

1

previous spread

1   Orange offerings. Asian shapes and figures combine to make an interesting monochromatic display. Work with one shade to create maximum visual impact.
2   Vietnamese market scene.
3   The lush and fertile Vietnamese countryside.
4   The grain of life. Vietnamese women traditionally carry out the back-breaking task of planting and harvesting the rice fields.
5   A Vietnamese woman along the Mekong Delta.
6   Orange inspirations. Traditional Southeast Asian symbols such as bamboo, frangipani and umbrellas are now available
    in contemporary designs, patterns and home decorations.
7   Wrapping paper with Asian motifs, colours and patterns could be used as placemats, to cover a side table or framed and admired for its beauty.
8   The non la cone-shaped Vietnamese hat is made from palm leaves and protects against the sun and rain. Its simple and beautiful design has
    become a widely-recognised symbol of Vietnam.

1   Low style dining. In typical Asian style, eating close to the floor is popular and enjoyed by all. Orange plates, coloured glass vases and a few
    accessories play up the Eastern influence with style.
2   The small Vietnamese sugar bowl shows the French colonial influence in local pottery design, where different coloured shades such as the green and
    red is a distinct departure from the more common blue and white. A contemporary melamine tiffin box (stackable lunchbox originally made of
    steel tin) is a modern interpretation of the East and West with new materials used in old ways.

2

3

4

Also linking these three countries is the Mekong River or the "mother of all rivers" in Laos, "the great river" in Cambodia and "the nine dragon river" in Vietnam. Originating in the Tibetan highland plateau, the river flows through China, Myanmar, Laos, Cambodia and the southern Vietnam before flowing into the South China Seas. The mighty Mekong River is a source of water for daily life, transportation, playground for children and rich source of food and sustainance for the people of these nations as it provides not only marine life but also a rich soil and water for growing fruit, vegetables and rice. The capital cities of Vientiane in Laos and Phnom Penh in Cambodia have the river flowing through its central part. Life along the Mekong continues to define this region and continues much like it has for hundreds of years with daily activities and business conducted along its banks.

1   *Lightly glazed black ceramic vases by Charlotte Cain are a modern contrast to the tropical environment, chartreuse table runner and carved table.*
2   *Light summer touches. Rattan placemats, brightly-coloured napkins and pretty accessories dress up any meal.*
3   *An ethnic collection of lacquer bowls and coasters from the region. Lacquer is an extremely distinctive, beautiful and traditional Asian handicraft that is used to make anything from offering vessels and betel boxes to placemats, serving bowls and picture frames. The process traditionally begins with a bamboo frame but for highest quality items horsehair, from the tail, is wrapped around the frame to give the bowl incredible flexibility and durability.*
4   *Fruit and vegetable market in Vietnam.*

1

2

Complex, yes, each of the three countries has its own distinguishing mix of ethnic and religious influences (Cambodia with the strongest Indian influence and large Khmer population; Laos more influenced by the Khmer, Vietnamese and Thai cultures; while Vietnam has strong cultural and historical links to China); unique, definitely for each has undisputable national identities and characteristics; similar, without a doubt. Not to contradict their uniqueness but because of their undeniable Buddhist beliefs, rituals, code of conduct, and the shared influences in their art and architecture and essentially because of the gentleness and shy hospitality of their people, these nations are similar and inspiring in the same manner.

Drawing inspiration from this region is not difficult. It's the serenity of the Buddhist monks, their magnificently coloured saffron robes, their splendid temples and inspiring rituals that remain with one. The peacefulness and purity of a Buddha image or statue and the gentleness of the local people. Appreciating the simple, basic aspects of objects – their symmetrical or even organic shape and their uplifting colour. The slower pace of life, an interdependency between family and society, a palpable antiquity and respect for the way things have always been done. A rich cultural and religious tradition which is admirable, combined with an enviable sense of simplicity.

previous spread

1   *Silky smooth seating. Contrasting silk-covered armchairs and sofa combine to create a strikingly modern and plush space.*
2   *Fluid two-toned ceramic vases make a gorgeous side display.*
3   *The tropical heliconia plant is known for its beautiful bright colours and petal like spikes.*

1   *The soft violet tone on the seat and cushions creates a soft, restful mood.*
2   *Cushions are an inexpensive, easy way to change any room. Look for colours, materials, designs, patterns that interest you and have fun changing them around and combining them in different ways for a quick, easy room make-over.*
3   *Peaceful dreams. Invigorating yet calming at the same time, this bedroom balances out the bright tones with a simple patterned bedspread, symmetry and the serene vibe of the monk painting overhead.*

Mongolia

Rustic and Vast

"Life in Mongolia is all about living with nature. It is about being completely in tune with our environment, our animals and our basic needs. Nature is all the inspiration we need."
– Narantsetseg, nomad.

"Are you wintering well?" "Are you spending this spring in peace?" These sincere and poetic sounding phrases are typical Mongolian greetings and say so much of the people and their outlook towards life. Peace is equivalent to happiness and hospitality. And friendliness is a tradition that is respected by all in this vast land where the hard conditions of life could create major isolation amongst the people. But it is not like that in Mongolia. Mongolians know how to lead a life of complete harmony with "mother nature" and under "father sky".

A landlocked country located in northern Asia, Mongolia is surrounded by China in the south and Russia to the north. One of the last unspoiled wilderness areas in Asia, Mongolian people are traditionally nomads and lead a life intimately connected with nature and the ways of the animals. Horses, cattle (including yaks), sheep, goats and camels are praised as the "five treasures" with horses being highly respected and considered the "emeralds". The relationship between Mongolians and horses is so deeply rooted that it seems impossible to view Mongolia's history without horses and certainly to understand Mongolian culture without them. The legendary 13th-century warrior Chinggis

Khaan established an empire that extended from Hungary to Korea and from Siberia to Tibet, all lead on horseback. As history has shown, the horse was his greatest weapon. The horse-mounted Mongol soldiers terrified their enemies; cities often surrendered upon the sighting of a single Mongol patrol. Even today, centuries later, horses are still used for travel, herding, hunting, sport and sustenance (both for horsemeat and mare's milk). Mongols have long been known as the best horsemen in Asia and small children learn to ride a horse by the time they are three or four. During the biggest national festival, Nadaam, everyone turns out on the open grasslands to participate in or to cheer on the popular sports of horse racing, archery and wrestling. The horse races are hugely popular with up to 1,000 horses participating in competitions that test the horse's skill, not the rider's. The top five winners are talked about and revered with poetry and music, and even the losing horse is serenaded with a song. It's no surprise then that in Mongolia, horses are equated with freedom and well-being.

While horses may be the national pride of Mongolia – unquestionably – the most identifiable symbol of Mongolia is their distinct dwelling. Ideally suited to their pastoral lifestyle and harsh terrain, the Mongolian people have been using for over 2,000 years a clever and collapsible home called a *ger* or *yurt* (*ger* is Mongolian for "home" and *yurta* is the Russian word that has become *yurt* in English).

Naturally graceful and powerful, the horse is highly regarded in many ancient cultures. In Mongolia, it is treasured and vital to the traditional nomadic lifestyle.

1   The open, vastness of a Buddhist monastery echoes Mongolia's landscape.

2   A traditional carpet weaver at work. Chinese designs and motifs are extremely popular in the intricate carpet patterns.

3   A quiet reading corner on the steppes. Doors and windows are often painted blue in praise of the sky and heavens.

4   A modern rustic ger. Cement walls offer a low-maintenance rough look that is softened with comfy large contemporary seating, a rice paper lantern and natural wood elements. The metal hooks on the ceiling are an original and creative way to deal with electrical circuitry, plus it makes for lots of wonderful lighting flexibility.

A *ger* is easily assembled and disassembled with its components designed to be loaded onto the back of camels or yaks. The wooden frame forms a circle that is then covered by large pieces of felt made from goat or camel hair. Its circular shape makes the *ger* resilient to Mongolia's strong winds while the layers of felt vary according to the season and provide a quick drying material against the rain and melting snow. The interior layout of the home is dictated by tradition and the heavens above. The fire for cooking and heat is placed in the centre of the *ger*, below the smoke-hole ring in the roof. The door always faces south in order to capture more sunlight in the windowless structure. Towards the back wall is the family altar with Buddhist images, family photos and suitcases. Near the altar and on the western side is the seat of honour for guests, with the host and family utilising the eastern side. The altar divides the *ger* into east and west. The eastern part of the home is used by the women for cooking, water buckets and for keeping theirs and their children's belongings. It is believed that the eastern side is looked after by the sun. The western side or the male side is believed to be protected by the heavens and is where the men's belongings, saddles and bridles, big leather bag containing *arkhi* (which is a light liquor distilled from cow's milk) and *airag* or the national drink made of fermented mare's milk are kept. Around the walls there are two or three low beds with cabinets and a small table and chairs is placed in the centre near the fire. Tradition also dictates a host of rules and etiquette for living and visiting a family in a *ger* that are second nature to Mongols but that outsiders should become acquainted with. But some things are obvious and clear, one never turns anyone away from their *ger* and there is always a cup of *airag* to greet the thirsty and tired guests.

1   *Beauty in the raw. A wooden tray displays an unusual assortment of pods, seeds, bark and sticks collected from nature walks.*
2   *Mongolians are big tea drinkers with their local version called suutei tsai or salty tea with milk.*
    Whatever your preference, indulge in the ancient restful, restorative ritual of drinking tea in style.

1

Mongolia has always had a defined artistic past with influences from all over the world. This was evident since the time of the Mongol empire of Chinggis Khaan and Khublai Khaan to the later days of Chinese occupation and Russian domination. Nevertheless, they have always remained pure to their aesthetic, only taking in minimal influences and rarely losing its unique identity. They love to decorate every item in their home, inside the *ger* and even on the trappings of their animals. With Tibetan Buddhism being the nation's predominant religion, the religion's auspicious motifs are popular decorating symbols. Everything from rugs, carpets, wall decorations and furniture is elevated from the common to the uncommon with inspiring designs. Mongolian furniture is recognised for its bright multi-coloured patterns commonly drawn on red and yellowish backgrounds – a seemingly sure way to inject warmth and a little peace and harmony to domestic life on the rugged steppes.

1   *Clothing has been made for centuries from wool, cowhide and other animal skins to protect from the rough weather and rugged terrain. Boots especially, are always well-insulated, comfortable, durable and an ideal artistic canvas.*
2   *On the nature trail. A Mongolian nomad and his horse. 40 per cent of the 2.4 million inhabitants are still nomadic herders.*
3   *The intricately embroidered and decorated headgear are ideally suited for display items.*
4   *The simple curves and variation of shapes, finish and detail on each stirrup makes for an original display. For a personal statement, proudly exhibit your collection of choice in appropriate shelving and space to maximise its visual appeal.*
5   *Local life is intimately connected with the ways of the animals and their images are popularly used for traditional games.*

1

1 A dark, solid-wood coffee-table serves double duty as an impromptu seating area with an assortment of low-level seating such as wooden stools, soft rugs and plenty of cushions. Earthy, browny-reddish tones pull it all together with style.
2 An antique Mongolian saddle is worthy of display and admiration for its exquisite workmanship.
3 Eastern dining in style. Hand-made ceramics and brass drinking vessels create a non-fussy yet elegant table setting.

2

3

overleaf

1   Laviran Temple at the Buddhist monastery of Erdene Zuu located in the ancient capital of Karakoram.
2   A traditional Tibetan thangka is intended to serve as a support for meditation, being a visual reminder of Buddhist teachings.
3   Plenty of dark wood set against a white background always looks alluring and comfortable. Punctuate the look with some soft, jewel toned cushions.
4   "Land of the blue sky" is no exaggeration in the vast, open Mongolian terrain. Traditional gers have withstood the test of time and are still the home of choice for the local people – even in the capital city where they are common sites in the outskirts of town.
5   One of the three Zuu temples at Erdene Zuu monastery.
6   Asian teapots are grouped to enhance the beauty and uniqueness of each piece, while playing up the Eastern look of the painted Tibetan cabinet.

2

3

It's precisely that "warmth" that we are after when putting together a Mongolian-inspired home. The modern day *ger* generates a warm and fuzzy feeling through plenty of tactile textures, soft materials and embracing colours. Even in a not-so-harsh climate, the cocooning and nesting instinct is within us all and whether it's the entire home or just the bedroom, a comfortable, sensual home does wonders in helping to restore one's inner balance and harmony. Create your own contemporary cosy dwelling with plenty of creature comforts such as furry, soft and natural materials – think rabbit fur, cashmere, cowhide, leather and suede. Combined with weather worn wood, some rustic iron and calming hues such as earthy brown, soft greys or natural clay tones and it's easy to create a modern *ger*-influenced home with all the comforts of today. The Mongolian nomadic lifestyle may be worlds away from today's fast-paced life but the human need to hide away, regenerate and relax in comfort at home is universal for all of us living under the big blue sky.

1   *Nesting instincts. Create an inviting bedroom with a large nature-inspired canvas, furry throw and plenty of cushions
     and light for snuggly reading. The ingenious tower book stand not only looks great but is also an amazing space saver.*
2   *Weathered, rustic wheels are popular for their uneven, natural charm as is the roughly-finished clay horse statue.*
3   *Antique leather trunks in various sizes look great together plus they provide plenty of stylish storage.
     A few small rice-baskets (used for measuring rice quantities) extend the rustic, natural feel.*

1   The expansive blue dome of sky that hangs over the entire country has given origin to its popular name "Blue Mongolia."
2   Nature-inspired and decorative items and table settings speak to the natural instincts in all of us.
    A few sculptural floral stems are always an inspirational starting point.
3   Close-up of cowhide seating and cushions.
4   The traditional nomadic lifestyle can still be found in the countryside and even in the capital city of Ulaanbaatar.
5   Create a rustic, nomadic inspired still-life of your own with similarly textured and finished items such as these warm and earthy pieces.

106

1 An urban ger. This home's charm (1&2) lies in its part-rustic, part-industrial feel that is created through the use of raw, untreated materials and surfaces. The dining area is modern and convivial with its moody dark hues and witty details.
2 A stainless-steel and cement kitchen is low-maintenance and durable.

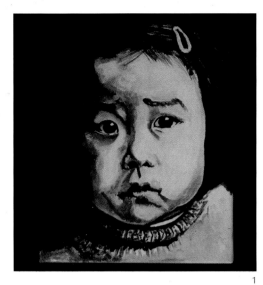

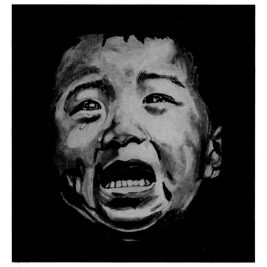

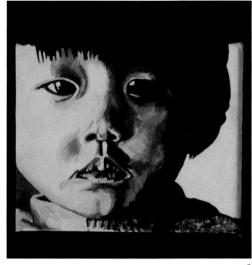

1,2&3   Asian faces painted in charcoal.
   4   Natural splendor. A patchwork wall of several wooden panels creates a sense of depth and richness to this bathroom.
   5   Alabaster toned ceramics are beautiful on their own and more impressive when paired up.
   6   Soft, snug seating is dramatised with overall dark hues and moody lighting.

1   *Fun, quirky pieces such as this porcelain gun-vase are an easy way to incorporate some fun and style into your home.*
2   *Sleek, comfy and stylish. A contemporary pairing of natural cowhide and chrome for the modern home.*

Thailand

Regal and Hip

"When I think of Thai style today, I think of foreign influences reinterpreted in an Asian way. There is usually some sanuk *or sense of fun and whimsy, mixed with Asian touches such as materials like coconut, bamboo or teak. All the while executed with grace." – Nawarat, journalist.*

It's been said that the cornerstone to Thai culture is their religion and their monarchy. This is definitely true and visibly apparent to anyone who has visited the country or knows a person of Thai origin. With approximately 95 per cent of the Thai population Buddhists, it is easy to understand the importance of the shrines, temples, Buddha images and the role they play in daily life. Along with their religion, the monarchy is a great source of pride, respect and sense of identity for the Thai people. The monarchy is also the driving force in the long, glorious history and conception of beauty, perfection and harmony in the refined arts and crafts. It puts the regal and the royal in Thailand. These are undoubtedly the cornerstones, but one more thing must be said about Thai culture and Thai people, they love beautiful things. That may sound like a strange statement, since yes, of course, people everywhere love beautiful things. But spend some time in Asia and then Thailand and you will begin to understand that statement. They know how to embellish, rework, pare down, combine and mix anything so that it looks refreshingly beautiful. Just think of how they can transform the common fruit or vegetable through the skillful use of a knife! Thai style is distinct, ornate and definitely not subtle. As the Thais have demonstrated for centuries, beauty has always been in the details and nuances and the more details and nuances that exist, the more beautiful something becomes.

But what makes Thai style so distinct? Definitely their religion, monarchy and appreciation for all things "beautiful" are guiding factors, but one other element is at play – the country's unique geography and history. Thailand really is the meeting place between two great Asian cultures – India and China. Its long rich history is imbued with Chinese, Indian and Khmer influences in everything from its language, music, theatre, dance, art and architecture to its similarities in traditional life due to common Asian beliefs and religion. This strong, deep Asian identity, combined with the fact that it is the only country in Southeast Asia never to have been taken over by a European power, has given Thais a different perspective. While its bordering neighbours Burma, Laos, Cambodia and Malaysia were slowly colonised by the British, Dutch and French, Thailand managed to keep the foreign forces at bay by the shrewd rulers King Mongkut (r.1851-1888) and his son King Chulalongkorn (r.1888-1910). Thailand was well on its way to nurturing its admirable ability to absorb outside influence without losing any if its identity.

History certainly gives us much hindsight and perspective, but the really interesting aspect is what is happening today. Modern contemporary tastes have converged with the time-honoured crafts, skills and aesthetic to create a thoroughly unique Thai style. The country has earned its place as a major design centre for modern furniture, lamps, vases and decorative items that are now exported and found in major shops around the world. Thais have mastered the art of creating things that are current, mod, hip and distinctly Asian. Some of the greatest showpieces of this look and style are the hotels and spas that have been recognised as some of the best in the world.

Buddha style. With so many beautiful interpretations of the Buddha image available now, look for one to suit your taste and style.
This meditative Buddha is painted on large wooden planks and is sure to become the focal point of any room.
Some contemporary acrylic stools and boxes add a modern touch and contrast.

When thinking of Thailand, its culture and its style, one image comes repeatedly to mind – the glowing, golden stupa domes of the wats or temple complexes. These elegant, soaring pointed towers dot the Thai landscape from urban centres to hilltops and white sandy beaches. Gold has been used by man, for centuries and throughout the world, to adorn religious icons and spaces for worship not only because gold is so precious, but also because gold is light. When applied to any surface a glistening, luminous effect is created. One of the most famous *wats* in Bangkok is the Wat Phra Kaeo or the Temple of the Emerald Buddha (the Emerald Buddha, made from jade, is the most venerated of all the thousand Buddha images in the country), serves as the royal chapel and is located within the spectacular Grand Palace compound. The Grand Palace is a glorious example of classical Thai architecture, detail, ornamentation and design. Thais love their gold and glitter, and whether they use it as a focal point or detail, it always manages to convey a hint of royal grandeur and elegance.

1   Royal grandeur. A golden statue poised in the gracefully and heartfelt Thai wai, or prayer-like salutation
     at the spectacular Grand Palace compound in Bangkok.
2   Impressively worked glass mosaic warriors adorn the outside of a structure in the Grand Palace.
3   More decorative statues line the architecture amidst the gold carvings, stucco, mosaic and jewel encrusted ornamentation.
4   An ornate and hand-painted mask used in the classic theatre style known as Khon (masked drama). Storylines are drawn
     from the Ramakien, the Thai version of the Indian Ramayana. Different coloured masks are used to depict the major characters
     with white representing Hanuman, the monkey god.

When it comes to colour, Thailand is a little like India in its riotous use of saturated colours in everything from food, architecture, clothing, textiles – you name it. In the Thai calendar there is even a colour assigned to each day of the week based on ancient Indian astrology and the corresponding gods of the planets. In Thailand, the colour of your birth day is traditionally considered more important than the actual date. It is no coincidence that the palette of red, yellow, pink, green, orange, sky blue and violet is often found at temples, boat prows, spirit house pedestals and other decorations. And although it is easy to draw inspiration from vivid combinations and tones, the following pages highlight a more restrained, lush and modern use of colour – colour used as a mood enhancer and ambiance creator. Something the Thais would most definitely approve of.

1   The beautiful worn, baroque look of the side table makes for a special display area. Mix high end boutique and market finds for a quirky, eclectic look e.g. tiered Thai box, cut crystal, glossy vases and lacquer plates.
2   A tapestry-like glass mosaic window decoration from the Grand Palace.
3   Lily pad-inspired floating votives are made out of pounded tin and can hold real flowers such as the pink lotuses or small candles.

5

6

7

1

To convey the look at home, play around with golden accents and sumptuous deep purples combined with neutral shades of black, grey and white. Go with whatever shade that moves you – scarlet, sapphire blue, any rich intense colour combined with something neutral, silky and metallic will create an alluring and completely modern space. If the feel is too dramatic for an overall look, it is easy to lighten up the mood by incorporating floral touches and interesting textures and surfaces.

Try out different shades and accessories and take a lesson from Thai designers who are so inspirational for their uninhibited use of old and new together, and ability to mix and not necessarily match. Look for the beauty in the old and new. They know how to recycle and transform in a fresh way while conversely creating the new to reinterpret the best of what's been done before with the best of what is hip now. It's a huge talent and it's definitely Thai.

previous spread

A shelf with a view. A resin Buddha statue sits serenely amidst a collection of glassware. If your china cabinet has visible shelves, group things by colour or shape and take time to add a few whimsical touches that will transform it from the ordinary to the extraordinary.

1   *Fit for a king. The common aluminum Thai rice taureen, tea pot and cups take on a royal flair with their raised ornamental surface worked to echo the gold patterns commonly found in palaces. Combine the everyday with something special for modern sophistication.*
2   *Flower power. Some pretty floral wallpaper immediately creates a special place. A selection of beautiful vases, treasured pieces and a few buds are all one needs to create an inspired arrangement.*

126

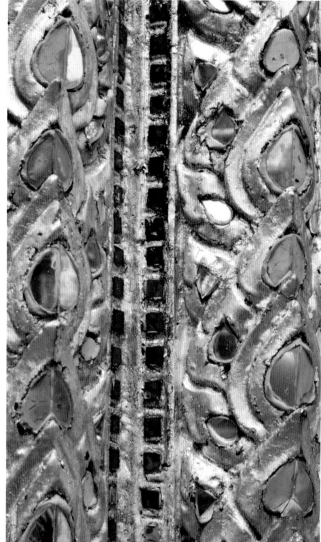

2

3

1   Sit down and have some fun. So much can be done to personalise a small seating area.
    The painting sets a modernist tone and the mirror side table, streamlined chair and reflective vases all beautifully
    execute the theme, while the balloon decorative rug adds a bit of fun and humour.
2   A little light magic. A gold lacquered lamp gives an instant glow to any corner. Coloured glassware is fun to collect because of the limitless
    designs, shapes and its luminous qualities – choose a colour theme and your personalised eclectic collection will always look great together.
3   Close-up of typical gold and glass patterning.

    overleaf

1   A splashing of gold leaves worked into the black lacquer transforms the common tray.
2   Digitally-printed Thai gift bags add a surreal Asian touch to the table.
3   The gold birdcage is reminiscent of the gold chedis of the Golden Palace. A birdcage makes a wonderful addition to any
    room either with something to display, or left empty and admired for its simple structure and design.
4   Close-up of cabbage rose flower petals.
5   Baubles and bowls. An eclectic, ethnic collection of gold and silver baubles, gold lacquered bowls, mercury glass candlesticks
    and highly ornate aluminum Thai drinking glasses, resting inside the wine glasses, combine magnificently for a dazzling occasion.

1

3

2

4

previous spread

1   Texture, texture, texture. Strips of leather fringe give amazing texture and personality to The Witch Chair by Tord Boontje. Set against a large
    silver textural painting and slick, reflective gold vases, the feel is completely luxurious and glamorous.
2   Close-up detail of the black and gold vase display. Beautiful glossy organic shapes are displayed to maximum effect on a glass and steel side table.

1   A royal retreat. A little drama goes a long way in creating an inviting and luxurious bedroom fit for a king and queen. Silky fabrics, silver and gold
    metallic cushions and dark walls elegantly and quietly create the decadent boudoir. And don't forget a few exotic orchid petals, sprinkled on the
    bed for an Asian touch.
2   A little black magic. A large, glossy, curvy room divider adds waves of style and sophistication to any corner. The rattan day bed plays up the
    dramatic mood with an antique golden throw and accessories while the bold, geometric lamp and painting in the background blend well with
    the dark tones of the decadent cushions, throw and accessories to convey a little mystery.

Japan

Ceremonial and Neon

"Japanese style is hard to define but easy to depict. Words to describe Japanese style – clean, pure, simple and spatial. How to spot it? Maybe more through the feeling it elicits rather than a look, a lightness, a purpose or a mood."
– Hikaru, marketing executive.

Zen, sushi, geisha, tatami, kimono...so foreign, yet so familiar. Japan is like that. On the surface level, it is easy for the foreigner to find some comfort in all the familiar references, popular food, national icons e.g. sumo wrestlers, geishas, *kabuki* actors but below all that we claim to "know," there is that undeniable feeling that one is only touching the surface. For below that surface is a mind boggling kaleidoscope of history, tradition, ceremony, and artistry alongside a cutting-edge pop culture wonderland of neon mega-this and micro-that. One thing is for sure, Japan does not bore.

Japanese legend recounts that this chain of several thousand islands was formed by the drops falling from the spear of the founding god as it was drawn from the ocean. From anywhere in the misty countryside, one can certainly sense the belief in this myth and begin to comprehend the relationship that exists among the mountains, ocean and its people. This relationship between nature and the Japanese people is paramount to understanding and appreciating their sense of design, artistry and beliefs. Shintoism the native animism, instilled in the Japanese people an unrivalled love and respect for nature in its tiniest, most simple form (a stone, a leaf). Nature is, after all, the original master of form, and Japanese *wabi sabi* design philosophy (respect for the intrinsic nature of materials) reflects this. It is a philosophy rooted in humility, simplicity, subtlety, restraint and the beauty in the allusion, asymmetrical, imperfect and impermanent quality of things and objects.

In the 12th century, *Ch'an* (Zen) Buddhism started its influence in Japan and its accent on simplicity merged perfectly with the deeply-embedded Shintoism that already existed in the people. The Japanese Zen belief also places keen importance to man's link with nature. The Zen spirit is emphasised through simplicity, purity and naturalness in one's surroundings, which in turn contribute to and shape one's peace of mind. Applying this belief to design terms, Zen favours the purity of natural materials and textures – the grain of the wood, the roughness of a stone or the curve of a branch. This subtlety is even evident in Zen's use of screens and sliding doors, which are much less obtrusive to an interior than a door. They also allow light in, another important area of the Zen aesthetic. Zen design may not be for everyone, but there is certainly a lot to be admired and respected for its pared down essence, discipline and orderliness. From an outsider and even Western point of view, it is simply amazing to see and necessary to acknowledge and to understand how the guiding philosophy, the ritual of the everyday and the ceremony of life's treasured moments has become embedded in Japanese culture and way of life. There is *wabi sabi* and Zen style when it comes to home decorating but there is also the famous tea ceremony or *cha-no-yu*, which has elevated the act of drinking tea to a time-honoured ritual based on the concept of *ichi-go ichi-e* or "one time, one meeting." Or in other terms, take time to fully appreciate your company and setting for this a unique moment in life's evanescent ways. When it comes to daily eating, there is *washoku* or "the harmony of food" and its guiding principles that bring nutritional balance and aesthetic harmony to the dining table. And even for something as whimsical and indulgent as flower arrangements the Japanese have *ikebana*. Unlike Western ways of arranging flowers, *ikebana* looks at the linear aspect of the arrangement not only through the flowers but also with vases, leaves, stems and branches.

Porcelain piggybanks reflect the Japanese respect for tradition combined with a modern quirkiness and sense of the unexpected.

1

1   The beauty of the bark. Nature is the original design master and the Japanese have appreciated and revered its form,
    subtleties and nuances for centuries.
2   A tachi-gata or pedestal stone lantern adds mystique, tradition and spirituality to the garden.
3   Simplicity of form. This marbled oval stoneware vessel by Chua Soo Khim is a beautiful example of the enduring appeal of simple form and design.
4   The Japanese chochin lantern is commonly found in shops and restaurants, and usually has a name or landscape printed on it.
5   Light the way. A collection of Asian lanterns are artfully displayed along a dark staircase. The lantern was originally introduced to Japan
    by the Chinese, and they were used to light doorways to shrines and temples.

Ikebana's entire purpose is to create points that symbolise heaven, earth and mankind. Flower arranging, yet another of life's pleasures, elevated to a philosophical level and appreciated with subdued modesty and refinement.

For the Japanese, less is more not only in architecture and clean living but also in their expertise of combining colours. Traditional and ceremonial Japanese garments are showpieces of sophisticated colour combinations and beauty – soft blue against a striking gold tone, for example. This sophistication is also beautifully exemplified in a variety of other art forms – flower arrangement, gardening, calligraphy and poetry. Taking a page from the keen Japanese appreciation of nature, a contemporary home can beautifully integrate Japanese elements through subdued colours and dark, natural wood. A logical colour choice is pine green – the colour of tranquility, harmony and rebirth. The beauty of a natural environment is always evoked with green and this fresh palette has the ability to graciously recede, allowing other shades to grow brighter in its presence. When paired with plum, it is restrained and elegant. A light, aquamarine blue is another shade that incorporates beautifully into many modern homes and serves as a serene background for more vibrant accessories and details. Look through photographs of detailed kimonos and textiles – inspiration will soon follow.

1   Inspirational blossoms. Cherry blossoms (sakura) are the "unofficial national flowers" of Japan. They are at full bloom for a few days in the spring and the entire country takes time to appreciate them in all their glory by either walking and looking, painting, taking photographs or having hanami parties or cherry blossom viewing parties and picnics under the trees.
2   These little emperor and princess decorations are typically used on March 3rd for the Hinamatsuri or Doll's Festival that celebrates the growth and happiness of young girls.
3   A deep plum man's kimono exemplifies simplicity and perfect form.
4   Sakura, a Japanese-inspired mixed media artwork by Lee Meiling transforms the bathroom in the the New Majestic Hotel (Singapore) into a fantasy and nature-inspired space through imagery, colour and texture.

1   *Still life to real life. Playing off the shape, purity and colour tones of the painting, a cotton branch and simple cylindrical, pastel vases and candles bring it all to real life.*

2   *The graceful lines and curves of the Japanese Buddhist temples are readily identifiable because of two main characteristics –*
they are remarkably well integrated with the natural environment, and their simplicity of structures and the building materials are
almost always wood, as opposed to stone. The stunning Kiyomizu-dera Temple (temple of pure water) in Kyoto is built on a
steep hillside, above a flowing waterfull and suspended on giant wooden pillars.

3   *Dating back to the 11ᵗʰ millennium BC, pottery is one of Japan's oldest art forms and among the earliest in the world.*
From rustic pottery to fine bone china, Japan has a wealth of styles and quality to suit everyone's taste.

4   *A peaceful, simple garden creates an instant retreat for meditation and relaxation.*

5   *Two geishas strike a pose in front of the long staircase leading to the three-storey pagoda of Kiyomizu-dera Temple.*

    overleaf

1   *A traditional thatched roof house in the countryside set amidst the understatement and simplicity of a typical Japanese garden.*

2   *The beauty of the grain – tree stumps become unique side tables with the addition of a circular opening and the natural finish of*
the grain. On the wall hangs a mixed media artwork of sliced plastic tubing, paint and rice grains.

3   *A street lantern echoes the shape of a temple roof, and creates a sharp contrast to the soft tones and purity of the cherry blossoms.*

4   *A modern Ikebana printed glass vanity table and glass table lamp by Knowles & Christou pays tribute to the delicate*
beauty of a single branch and blossoms.

4

5

1   The glory of the maple tree. Like the springtime Cherry blossoms, the turning of the autumn leaves is cause for celebration and leaf viewing trips.
2   Traditional Japanese drummers play an important role in many festivals and folk art.
3   An iron four poster bed makes an ideal hanging spot for a man's treasured kimono.
    The bold and colourful cushions in spirit-lifting blooms give the room an additional eastern boost.
4   Beautiful textiles such as an obi, or kimono belt, can be used to dress up a bookcase, table or even a bed.
    Made of woven or dyed material and varying widely in colour, design, width and length, an obi is an easy way
    to incorporate some Japanese chic to any modern home.
5   A delicate balance. Look for simple and subtle items and design that will add a Japanese feel to your home.

overleaf

1   Block printing is another traditional Japanese art form and this modern reproduction of Utamaro, highly regarded as one of the foremost
    painters of beauty and of the ukiyoe form of block printing, was banned in the 18th century (when it first appeared)
    because of the intensity of its raw emotion.
2   Doll-making is traditional folk art in Japan. The kokeshi dolls are easily identifiable because of their wooden cylindrical body, round head,
    hand-painted design and soft, glossy finish. Kokeshi dolls are given as tokens to loved ones and make a hip alternative to traditional figurines.
3   Asian characters are universally appealing. Japanese characters lend an immediate exotic air to an old pharmacy sign.
    Antique shop signs and even street signs add a unique dose of history, culture and interest to contemporary homes – look for signboards in flea
    markets, shops and secondhand stores.
4   A mixed-media canvas by artist Ivan Lam dominates this contemporary dining area.

登録商標　血

大阪細菌研究所製品

特約店

ヒラヤ薬局

1

2

3

4

5

6

7

8

1

7

3

previous spread

1   Japan has a huge fascination with all things "cute," think Hello Kitty and Pikachu. In Japan the word for cute is kawaii and it has even become a recognisable term associated with Japanese pop culture.
2   The Sweetie pouf by Tord Boontje is a modern classic in its simple form, function and nature inspired fantasy design.
3   Powerful street graphics are art in themselves.
4   A typical action-packed Tokyo intersection. Neon signs, flashing billboards, a sea of people alongside order, youthful funk and traditional modesty.
5   Tord Boontje's delicate play with nature makes a fascinating backdrop to a simple bamboo patterned rice paper lantern and white tripod vase.
6   Like major cities around the world, Tokyo has a thriving youth culture and style that defines the moment.
7   Robots, electronics, computers – if you want what is cutting-edge look towards Japan.
8   Toy Story. Lighten things up with cute and quirky neon-tinged accessories.

1   Layer shades of plum, tea and leaf green for a restful sleep zone. Earthy tones and natural materials are conducive to relaxation and peace of mind.
    A string of maple leaves personalises the headboard and adds a wonderful decorative flourish.
2   Warriors have always been respected and revered across cultures and time.
3   A typical Japanese sitting area with tatami mats and sliding screens creates a peaceful sanctuary to enjoy tranquility and relaxation.

1

2

3

4

人生得意須盡歡

莫待金樽空對月

天生我才必有用

1

2

3

previous spread

1   Playing peek-a-boo amidst the display. Combine items based on colour, form texture and height
    to make an interesting collection of your favourite things.
2   Look East for geisha style and exotic decorating ideas.
3   Be inspired by Japanese appreciation and love for nature and learn to incorporate its influence in your home through
    seasonal plants and flowers, textiles and materials.
4   A large, glass panel cabinet by designers Knowles & Christou is transformed by the feminine blossoms and smooth finish of the materials.
5   Traditional seating in the Japanese home has always been low to the ground and consequently, their furniture was also designed low
    to the ground from tables and seating to cabinets and futons for sleeping. Balance the look with some tall, long items such as these
    calligraphy hangings or some tall plants such as bamboo.

1&2 Quality produce and seasonal eating are of prime importance to the Japanese people. Local markets are still popular and provide
     a wonderful insight into the local culture.
3   Restaurants often specialise in one dish and people flock to enjoy them.
4   A simple table setting for two. For the Japanese, presentation is everything when it comes to food.
     Look for the ideal serving plate and dishes that will enhance the food and thereby the entire eating experience.
     In the background hangs a young boy's kimono.

1

2

3

The importance of textiles in creating a personalised, Japanese-inspired space cannot be emphasised enough.Thank goodness that today, it is not only possible to find authentic textiles overseas but also, modern design has beautifully reinvented and popularised exotic Asian florals. Incorporate some timeless cherry blossom wallpaper or a chrysanthemum print cushion to your seating area. Japan is particularly rich in symbolic flower images and it's surprising to see how quickly one blossom can alter the mood in a room and evoke images of Japan. The chrysanthemum has been the traditional crest of the Imperial family since the 12th century – it represents happiness and longevity. Others include the cherry blossom, which denotes prosperity and riches; the

peach blossom, which stands for spring and marriage; and the peony, which symbolises marriage and fertility. Now, fast-forward to the present day Japan, home to the avant-garde and current day trends. Think neon flashing signs, robots, electronics and all things futuristic. It's a fascinating contrast to the discreet and ceremonious ways of the past, yet these two extremes co-exist beautifully. They are both undeniably Japanese in look and style and the rest of the world has openly embraced it. It's almost as if the young and old, but especially the young, seek entertainment and escapism from the frantic pace of daily life. From Godzilla, to Nintendo, anime and manga animation, Hello Kitty to Ultra Man, karaoke, J-Pop and funky schoolgirl fashion. If you want to see tradition and what is cool, look towards Japan.

1   *A cluster of beauty. Refined ceramics by Rina Menardi are inspiring in their lightness of colour and shape. The matte, yet still luminescent turquoise,*
      peridot, amethyst and topaz tones effortlessly complement each other and further enhance the simple lines of the ceramics.
2   *Gather small serving vessels and have fun with individual stems or leaves. Multiples of the same object are a great way to bring*
      a sense of harmony and order to a tabletop.
3   *The pure gemstone colours of the plates and their sinuous curves create an inviting tabletop.*

Philippines

Sunny and Laidback

"In the Philippines we have the traditional greeting Mabuhay, *which means many things – to live, to life, welcome or congratulations. It's that warm embrace of life that comes to mind when I think of my country. Filipino style comes from that happy spirit in the form of bright colours, bright prints and lots of soulful creativity." – Miriam, public relations manager.*

To even begin to understand the soul and creativity of the Filipino people, one has to begin with the country's unique history. The Philippines is an archipelago of over 7,000 islands in the South China Sea that came to the attention of the West when Portuguese explorer Ferdinand Magellan landed in 1521. Although Magellan was unsuccessful in claiming the land, he died in a bloody battle with local chieftain Lapu-Lapu, he paved the way for the Spanish who later returned and named the islands after the prince who would go on to become King Philip II. By 1571, the entire country, except the strictly Islamic Sulu archipelago, was under Spanish control.

The islands had been inhabited for thousands of years before Magellan, with a mix of indigenous people known as *Negritos* and early traders and immigrants from nearby Malaysia, China and Indonesia. But without a formal local form of government and with most of the population having no religion other than animism or nature worship practiced by their ancestors, the local people were very susceptible to new influences. Because of these unique circumstances, the Spanish were widely success-

ful in converting the local people to Christianity and today, the Philippines is the only predominantly Christian nation in Asia. Almost every town in the Philippines is dominated by a baroque church. The great folk fiestas, attended by hundreds of participants would seem typical of many other Asian festivals except the images that are carried are those of Spanish saints.

Three centuries of Spanish rule also left an indelible mark in the local language that is peppered with Spanish words, the cuisine that is a mix of Malay, Chinese and Spanish influences and the happy go-lucky *mañana* attitude of the Latin culture. After the Spanish left, the arrival of the Americans from 1898 to 1936 gave the Philippines the dubious honour of becoming the only Asian country to be colonised twice. Although the American period was short in comparison to the years the Spanish spent controlling the islands, the Americans also left their mark. Notable among them are an emphasis on education and the prevalence of English. Literacy is almost 93 per cent and one of the highest in Southeast Asia. There are 77 native languages, of which Tagalog is the basis of the national language, Filipino. But English is taught in schools as the universal second language and everybody speaks at least a touch of it. And yes, the other ubiquitous reminder of the American era is the GI Jeep, locally called "jeepney", left from the war. They are now the most popular form of public transportation and showcase for Filipino artistry and pop art – just one prime example of Filipino ingenuity and flair.

The only predominantly Christian nation in Asia, the Philippines is a glorious mix of Eastern roots and Western influences.

1   Children in the province hanging out and enjoying a lazy afternoon.
2   A portrait of a lady dressed in the national costume, the Maria Clara. Finely worked piña cloth
    and the pañuelo, or shoulder shawl, are typical trademarks of this delicate and feminine ensemble.
3   A colourful collection of boats adds charm to the sandy coastline.
4   The jeepney is folkart on wheels. Leftover jeeps from the American GIs have been reworked with
    Filipino ingenuity and are the principal source of public transportation, especially in major cities.
5   Close-up detail of embroidered piña cloth handkerchiefs and accessories commonly used with the national costume.

2

3

The easygoing charm of the Filipino people is well recognised in Asia. Nurtured by a tropical environment and their unique historical development, their natural sense of song, dance and hospitality shines in the region. The arrival of the Spanish brought an entirely new way of expressing music and with it, a new set of instruments such as the guitar, violin, piano and even the harp, that found their way into the Filipino people's lives. The American period greatly popularised Western music and although today, traditional tribal music is cherished, it is the international rock and pop that dominate popular culture.

Traditional Filipino dance styles originate from pre-Hispanic practices and are based largely on the agriculture cycle. Many stylise rice planting or harvesting, fishing or hunting, while others enact scenes from epic stories and traditional tribal rites and ceremonies. It is most common today that these tribal dance forms be performed alongside others derived from Spanish and American eras. These dances are performed in European style and dress. Dance being another example of the eclectic mix of contrasting styles from the East and West, integrated into what is now a Filipino style.

1   *The brilliant combination of sunny yellow and intense, midnight blue makes for a dramatic display.*
     Coloured glass is not only a beautiful art form but a fantastic way to incorporate some powerful shades and style to a room.
2   *A pious people, Filipinos are also known for their strong family ties, hometown loyalty and cockeyed optimism.*
3   *Forest friendly. Indigenous and incredibly beautiful materials such as bamboo, coconut and shapely grained woods are a natural*
     way to create a laidback, tropical space.

1

1   Hand-decorated coconut wood plates are eye-catching and versatile.
2   Bring in nature. Not much can compete with the pure form and beauty of fruits, flowers and plants. Enjoy what is easily available and in season.
    These buta-buta seeds are inedible but their vivid apple green skin and smooth shape are perfect for a decorative basket.
3   The coconut tree is known locally as "the tree of life" and with obvious reason. Every part of it is used, nothing wasted. The coconut's durable shell is
    ideal for items such as serving spoons and eating spoons.

1

2

3

4

5

The field of furniture design and handicrafts is another form of art where Filipino style shines and excels. Innovative design and world class furniture has been coming out of the Cebu province for years now that they are even known internationally for the "Cebu look" – the look being design driven with exquisite construction, finishing and originality. Growing tourism has created a new market for items that are still in daily use among rural peoples such as beautifully woven basketry products like bags and rice containers to trays and floor mats. Colourful woven clothes from the mountain people of the Cordillera Central produce distinctive textiles. A growing export market of well-made handicrafts in everything from Capiz shells and bamboo, wicker, coconut wood and textiles is bringing a well-recognised name in

quality and creativity to the country. However, the most widely-recognised textile from the Philippines is the *piña* cloth – a gossamer thin textile hand-loomed from the leaves of the pineapple plant. The pineapple by the way, native to Brazil, was brought by the Spanish but early evidence shows that the locals were already weaving cloths from other plants such as the banana and *abaca* (Manila hemp) plant. This delicate and treasured textile is favoured for the *Barong Tagalog* – the national attire of men used in weddings and other formal events. In yet another example of the mixing between Spanish influences and the local traditions, the *piña* cloth became customised with Spanish lace and embroidery patterns but completed with local ingenuity and flair.

1   With over 7,000 islands strewn between the South China Sea and the Pacific Ocean, the Philippines is known for its pristine beaches and rich diversity of marine life. Outrigger boats such as this are used for fishing and dot the coastline.

2, 3&4   Reef protection and fishing controls have ensured a healthy population of large reef fish, and great diversity in the underwater wilderness. The Philippines offers a magnificent spectacle for divers.

5   Hot tropics. Turn up the heat with some tropical inspiration in the form of bright botanical prints, flashes of hot colour, and plenty of bamboo and wicker elements such as baskets and woven floor mats.

6   Exotic tropical fruits and a portable straw mat are all that is required for a grand outdoor treat.

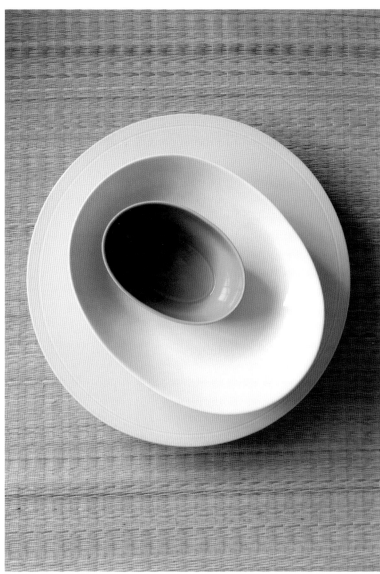

1

2

The coconut tree is not surprisingly called "the tree of life" in the Philippines. Every part of the tree is used for everything including food, shelter, fuel, handicrafts, household products, you name it. Their presence is an integral part of the Filipino scenery and life. After all, what would the sight of a glistening white sandy beach be without the sultry shadow of the coconut tree? The Philippine's idyllic coastline is by far the greatest attraction for visitors to the archipelago's 7,101 islands. Warm waters and coral reefs are a paradise for divers and have helped to put the Philippines on the world map for diving, beaches and tropical adventure. Channeling some of the Philippines tropical zest and vivacious spirit comes naturally in the form of bright colours such as canary yellow and fresh lime. Because of their insatiable cheeriness, bright hues

work best in large home spaces when contrasted against more subdued shades such as a relaxing sky or cobalt blue. A sure fire way to obtain a natural style is to mimic the elements – sunny yellow with sand, earth and stone hued pieces. Set dark rich wood against white walls for an airy, breezy feel. Match your accessories with the natural materials of your flooring or furniture for an easy, seamless look. Lots of materials in curvy shapes such as wicker, straw, bamboo and coconut are nice to the touch and look great. Lift your mood with fabulous greenery and plants. It's the ease, the comfort and the relaxed pace of life in the tropics that is so enticing. Nothing fussy, plenty of natural light and lots of eco-friendly materials paired with tropical enthusiastic shades and you're there – *Mabuhay* the Philippines.

1   *Form, function and taste. Svelte, extra-long green beans are as beautiful as they are delicious and popular in Southeast Asian cuisine.*
2   *Sunny yellow is often associated with celebration and symbolises hope. Look for the right tone and colour match to suit your space and personality, yet undeniably, yellow is optimistic and playful. Have fun with it.*
3   *The global kitchen. A collection of hand-woven baskets and trays gathered from exotic journeys add loads of personality to this kitchen window.*

1   Sunny break. Ethnic pieces such as this seashell decorated basket and woven display tray are real standouts when combined with contemporary tableware.
2   Look for unique hand-made pieces such as these ceramic pitchers that add charm and character to common household items.

1

1	A teak four poster bed plays up its jungle allure with vivid shades of green and uplifting prints.
2	Bring the outdoors in. If you have a lush garden, maximise the view with lots of large windows and open doors;
	or select a few large plants that will convey the relaxing greenery of the tropics; or fake the look with the
	wide selection of photo mural wallpaper available on or make your own with blown-up holiday snaps.
3	Whimsical flower cushions lend a fun and happy twist to this geometric pair of Ming style chairs.

2

3

overleaf

Playfully robust and expressive statues would be a surefire hit in any space.

Indonesia

Traditional and Artesian

"We are artists at heart and have grown up in an environment where we see the artisans at work, appreciate the workmanship and live with these traditional elements as part of our daily life. Indonesian style, like style everywhere, is moving forward and becoming more modern but for us, I don't think we can stray too far from our artesian traditions. It's part of our national identity." – Ardani, jewellery designer.

Indonesia is the definition of an exotic land, a mystical land, a land rich in traditions, religion and diversity. Comprising somewhere between 14,000 to 16,000 islands (depending on whether it is low or high tide) and located in the prime gateway between Western and Eastern sea trade, Indonesia has a history steeped with influences from explorers, invaders and colonists. With such a complicated history, it comes as no surprise that the national motto is "unity in diversity." To better illustrate, Indonesia is a tropical country, its predominant religion is Islam, its middle-class is Chinese, its official language is Bahasa Indonesia, its architecture has a strong Dutch colonial influence and its ancient monuments were built to both Buddhist and Hindu gods.

For the people of *Nusantara* ("the land between the waters", which is what Indonesians call their country), despite the various outside influences, their life continues to be rooted in the power of their land (nearly all of the country's islands are volcanic and the overwhelming majority of them active), their religion, their family, their spirits (they are great believers in the power of spirits – demons, ghosts, gods, and ancestors) and their art. Indisputably, there is one revered art form that encapsulates these influences and defines the Indonesian people, their culture and their spirit – *batik*.

The roots of *batik* date back through time and can be traced to several regions in Africa, India and other Southeast Asian countries, but the *batik* in Indonesia is unique and unequalled.

The centre of this art is Central Java in cities like Yogyakarta, Surakarta, Cirebon, Pekalongan and Indramayu. Nobody knows exactly when and where people started applying mud, vegetable paste, paraffin and wax to cloth that would resist a dye but today, traditional Indonesian *batik* is made by hand applying hot, liquid wax with a wooden pen or "canting" to a piece of undyed cloth. Some *batik* artists draw from memory, others wax over faint charcoal lines. The mark of a truly fine piece of *batik* is when the cloth has been waxed on both sides, and the design is as bright and clear on one side as it is on the other. The laborious process of waxing, dyeing, melting the wax, removing it and then redoing the entire process to achieve a multi-coloured intricate pattern can take the finest artisans 12 months or more to complete a single piece of a metre or two. Today, much of the *batik* used in Indonesia is produced in factories but the traditional art and pride involved in creating this artistic cloth can still be found, especially in Central Java.

This quintessential Indonesian textile is wrapped in symbolism, meaning and heritage. The flower motifs, twinning plants, birds, butterflies, fish, insects and geometric forms are rich in association and variety. The Buddhist (lotus flower), Hindu (interlocking and intersecting circular designs), Islamic (flat arabesques and calligraphy), Chinese (flying phoenix, two opposing dragons and soft pastel shaded colours), Malay (sweet perfumed flowers such as gardenia and jasmine, cucumber seeds and mangosteen calyx) and local influence is apparent in the patterns and colour choice. The design is certainly a salient attribute of *batik* but the other equally important factor is the dyeing technique. Local water and plant species greatly affected the shades of colour that were possible and consequently, each region of Java has its own characteristic tints. Among the many colours found in Javanese *batik*, four are definitely the most popular. There is indigo, the oldest and most popular; dark red; yellow; and the deep, rich Javanese somber brown known as soga brown, the dye is derived from the bark of the local soga tree.

A Wayang Golek hand-made puppet in traditional Central Javanese court dress and batik sarong.

Local tradition dictates its many uses from the everyday and widely popular *sarong* to flags, banners or wall hangings to being an important part of a girl's trousseau. This fabled cloth also has strong royal connections with some designs reserved for ceremonial royal occasions in the courts of Central Java. There is even meaning in the way a piece of *batik* cloth is folded, presented, worn and placed. But much like the meaning of the motifs and colour, the significance of a pattern will vary from workshop to workshop, region to region. Meanings are many and varied but all *batik* is filled with pride and national identity. Today it is possible to find *batik*-inspired prints on tablecloths, curtains, cushions, Western style clothing and many other household items. Its exotic appeal is too far-reaching to contain.

Indonesians are expressive people and they have become masters not only in the art of *batik*-making but also in the fields of dance, painting, sculpture and puppetry to name just a few. It is commonly said that in the island of Bali everyone is an artist. Ask around, it's true. The hotel receptionist, the taxi driver, the shopkeeper, they all possess enviable talent in some local form of artistic expression that has most likely been passed down from their parents and it will continue to be passed along to their children. Artistic flair is so closely interwoven with religious rituals that it seems a way of life for Indonesians. In Bali, a small island where 95 per cent of the people are Hindu, even the statues have fresh hibiscus flowers tucked behind their ears, a *batik sarong* and a colourful umbrella to hold.

1   *The beautiful and prolific tropical banana tree.*
2   *A white seating area serves as the perfect canvas for some colour therapy.*
     Gorgeous shades of leafy, jungle greens and bold floral prints liven up this living room.
3   *A neatly framed trio of masks from Bali.*
4   *Rattan and teak outdoor furniture is durable enough to withstand the elements yet comfortable enough to encourage plenty of use.*

previous spread

1   Create a global tapestry of your life. In this home carpets, favourite prints, textiles, door hangings and even an ornate umbrella
    are combined in daring and bold ways to create a highly personalised space. Artwork by Pacita Abad.
2   Maxi pattern living. Pattern on pattern on pattern works when the colours are coherent such as in this violet toned seating area.
    The glass plates on the coffee-table and large painting on the back wall are by the late Filipina artist, Pacita Abad.

1   Personalise your furniture with a favourite cloth or pattern. Here a display cabinet is covered in Indonesian batik
    and becomes the perfect complement for the batik-inspired dinnerware by Pacita Abad.
2   Hand-dyed yarns have a beauty, sheen and tone all their own.
3   Cast iron blocks used for cloth printing.

2

3

overleaf

1   Puppets have been used for centuries in Indonesia to tell the ancient Hindu epics of the Ramayana and Mahabarata, as well as ancient myths.
     Their delicate expressions and fine craftsmanship make an ideal decorative element.
2   Wayang Dinnerware by Pacita Abad pays tribute to the many colourful characters of the Ramayana and its Indonesian
     interpretation through shadow puppets.

185

Fresh *banten* (basket-like tray) are woven daily from coconut tree leaves, filled with flower petals and a few grains of rice. These *bantens* are placed outside shops, homes, hotels. The *bantens* are offered with lighted incense and offered to Batara Brahma, God of Fire.

More is more. This is the unwritten motto for traditional Indonesian art forms. The beauty of batiks comes from the infinite detail and colours apparent in a single metre of cloth. Traditional Bali *Pengosekan*-style paintings are covered to the borders in flora and fauna, people and gods.

1   A colourful sense of the tropics and the exotic is immediately evoked with this inspired staircase. The sea blue and contrasting lime green wall serve as the backdrop to a collection of colourful paintings, beaded boxes, cloth covered vase and woven suzani blanket covering the sidetable.
2   Tribal art – a tribal cushion holder is both practical and charming with its curved lines and natural finish.
     While the large carved doors on the stairway landing contrast beautifully with the clean surroundings.
3   Tropical comfort – this seating area is a wonderful mix of tropical colours such as lime, leafy green combined with urban black.
     The rattan antique daybed looks cool and inviting set agains bright, white walls and green accents.
4   Hand-carved wooden trays are representative of the art style of the Toraja people from the Indonesian island of Sulawesi.

1

2

3

1   Unique hand-made crafts abound in Indonesia. Traditional Balinese dancers are carved and hand-painted from a small piece
     of wood and highly appreciated for their minute attention to detail.
2   Carved detailing from a teak canopy bed.
3   A collection of Indonesian masks. Masks were widely used in the past to communicate with ancestors, for blessing of harvests,
     protection from great evil spirits, or to acquire new powers or new personalities.
4   Combine favourite prints and patterns for a highly original and ethnic sideboard. Beaded bracelets collected from global
     travel decorate the candlesticks atop a batik-covered sideboard. The batik collage on the wall, Hey Sugar, is by Pacita Abad.

1

Intricately carved woodwork decorates homes. Elaborately worked stone gates greet worshippers at the temple. And the hand-made puppets used in *Wayang Golek* are outfitted in head to toe finery and details to rival any real princess. The skill, patience and experience of the artisan are always visible. Indonesian style is a natural fit in a warm, tropical setting. "Bali Style" today instantly connotes the island breeze, swaying palm leaves and relaxed yet hip lounging that the island has so per-fected. A feeling of slow-down, enjoy the warmth of the sun and the beauty in all things great and small. But if you do not live in a tropical climate, don't shy away from using some traditional Indonesian elements in your home. Intersperse some *batik* cush-ions in your seating area, or a woven textile to snuggle in while watching TV, or some mango wood vases, or woven baskets – something natural, warm and beautiful. What home wouldn't want some of that? Like Indonesia, it's all in the mix.

1   A non-conventional background, such as this petrified piece of wood, creates a spectacular backdrop to a display
     inspired by its smooth texture and warm tones.
2   An exotic array of natural dye sources such as tree and plant bark, roots and seeds.

1   *Create a natural hideout within your home with an oversized, elaborate daybed complete with built-in shelves and magnificent carvings.*
2   *A teak canoe is brought out of the water and into the modern home with some ingenuity and brightly-coloured accessories.*
3   *The idyllic beaches of Indonesia.*
4   *Simply decorated paddles enhance but do not compete with the beauty of the wood's grain.*

2

3

4

2

3

1 Tribal artwork is highly appreciated for its symbolism and primitive characteristics.
2 Vintage items such as this brass fan are still popular today and blend in well with either traditional or contemporary homes.
3 Play with texture and different surfaces to balance the feel of your home. The cold cement wall is softened by the warmth of wooden table, while contrasting sharply with the rough look of the natural poles and the smoothness of the decorative items.

Index

Thanks to the following shops and artists/designers for lending us props and locations:

AkaMotif Indonesian Shop – (65) 6738-2996
Aliya – www.aliyastore.net
Arka Indonesian Shop – (65) 6737-9228
At Home Chez Choupinette – contact Agnès Verrier, at-home@choupinette.com.sg or (65)9769-4246
Blue Canopy – www.blue-canopy.com
Charlotte Cain ceramics – www.charlotte-cain-ceramics.com
Colin Seah, Ministry of Design – www.modonline.com
Cyclo – Vietnamese lacquerware – contact Janet (65) 9619-6059
Esme Living Colour Design – www.esmelivingcolour.com
FairPrice Antique – www.fairpriceantique.com
Hugo Kitchen Pte Ltd – (65) 6336-8898
Inspired by Leslie – www.inspiredbyleslie.net
Ketna Patel – www.ketnapatel.com
Lava East & Company Pte Ltd – www.lavaeast.com
Lims Arts & Living – (65) 6467-1300
Mod•Living – www.modliving.com.sg
New Majestic Hotel – www.newmajestichotel.com
Pacita Abad Art – www.pacitaabad.com
Pagado House – www.pagodahouse.com
Prettyfreakyfantasy – contact Idris Johor, prettyfreakyfantasy@yahoo.com.sg
Space Furniture – www.spacefurniture.com
Systemind Platform – www.systemindplatform.com
Takaraya – Japanese Touches for the home – contact Hiroko (65) 9796-8760
The Touch – www.thetouch.com.sg
Vanilla Home – www.vanilla-home.com
Ziegler Shoes- www.zieglershoes.com.sg

Acknowledgements

Thank you to the following people who provided us with their inspiring travel photographs:
Kelley Cheng, Mie Ingerslev, Thomas and Joyce Riber Knudsen, Michel and Adelien Vandeweghe,
Laura Tommasi, Jannie Walschot, Vicky Tapiador, and Ellen Nepilly

Hanneke Mennens – http://web.mac.com/m2.photography
Oksana Perkins – www.pbase.com/oksana_p
Alan Lee – www.mekongpicturehouse.com

A special thank you to the homeowners and friends: Marión and Sanjay Bhasin, Helle and John Espersen, Jennifer and André Levesque, Tina and Lou Milicevic, Charlotte and Bill Cain, Esme and Yuwa Hedrick-Wong, Jette Roggenbach, Mette Galst, Linda Jeffs and Mike Whanau, Lynda and Lloyd Darby, Barbara and Roberto Cristiani, Ketna Patel and Jonathan Reading, Jack and Kristiyani Garrity, Leslie Lim, Bitten and Heine Askjær, Chris Jaques, Jaye Sun, Kee and David Cronin, Lisa and Dan McHugh, Kam and Michael Koefed, Anuradha and Rahul Mathur, Nene and Lars Amstrup, Jennifer Villareal, Wendy and Steve Gardner, Joy and Colin Seah, Idris Johor and Jay Hammond, Sandhya Rupani and Agnès and Laurent Verrier.

A special thanks to my team – Marión Bravo-Bhasin for writing this book so wonderfully and making it all so very interesting and for all her support in everything we do; to the great photographers Alan Lee and Edward Hendricks for working such long hours and never being impatient; and to all at Page One who believed in this project and guided us in the right direction – the graphic designer Frédéric, and the editors Serena and Kelley. Lastly, I would like to thank my family – Jens, Nikolas and Rebekka – for their love and support.

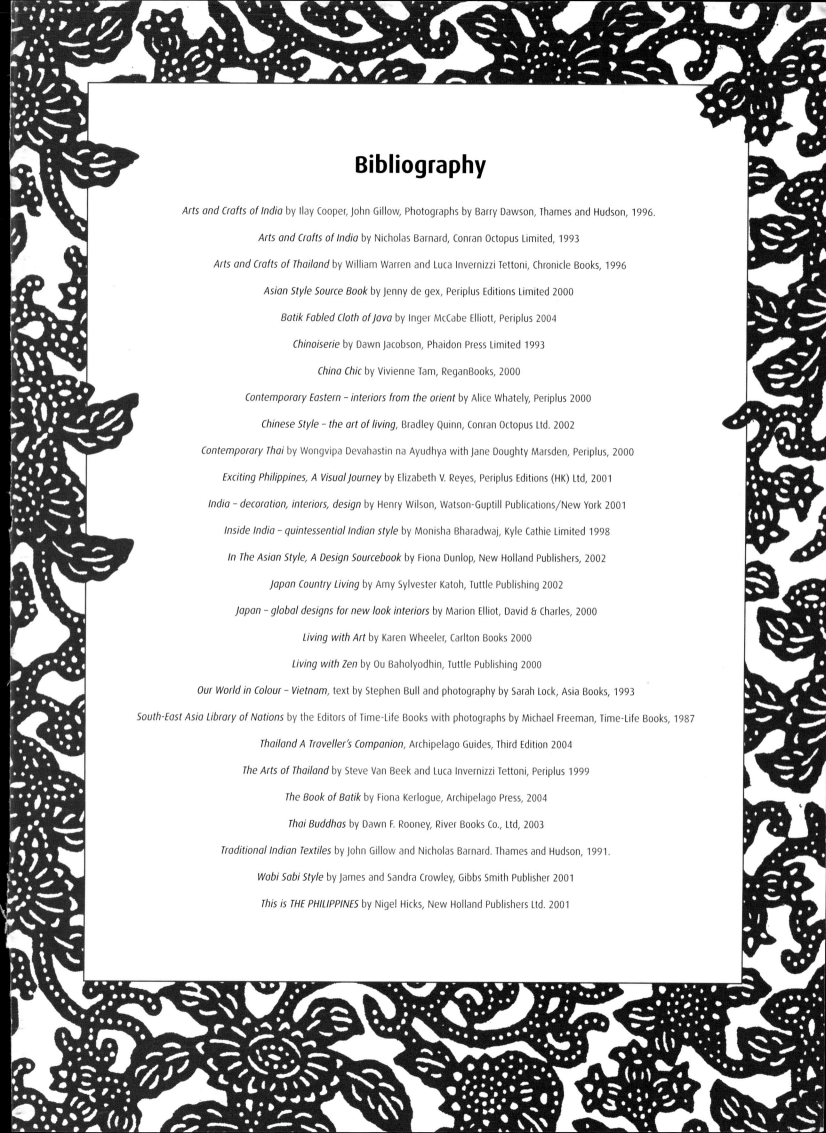

Bibliography

Arts and Crafts of India by Ilay Cooper, John Gillow, Photographs by Barry Dawson, Thames and Hudson, 1996.

Arts and Crafts of India by Nicholas Barnard, Conran Octopus Limited, 1993

Arts and Crafts of Thailand by William Warren and Luca Invernizzi Tettoni, Chronicle Books, 1996

Asian Style Source Book by Jenny de gex, Periplus Editions Limited 2000

Batik Fabled Cloth of Java by Inger McCabe Elliott, Periplus 2004

Chinoiserie by Dawn Jacobson, Phaidon Press Limited 1993

China Chic by Vivienne Tam, ReganBooks, 2000

Contemporary Eastern – interiors from the orient by Alice Whately, Periplus 2000

Chinese Style – the art of living, Bradley Quinn, Conran Octopus Ltd. 2002

Contemporary Thai by Wongvipa Devahastin na Ayudhya with Jane Doughty Marsden, Periplus, 2000

Exciting Philippines, A Visual Journey by Elizabeth V. Reyes, Periplus Editions (HK) Ltd, 2001

India – decoration, interiors, design by Henry Wilson, Watson-Guptill Publications/New York 2001

Inside India – quintessential Indian style by Monisha Bharadwaj, Kyle Cathie Limited 1998

In The Asian Style, A Design Sourcebook by Fiona Dunlop, New Holland Publishers, 2002

Japan Country Living by Amy Sylvester Katoh, Tuttle Publishing 2002

Japan – global designs for new look interiors by Marion Elliot, David & Charles, 2000

Living with Art by Karen Wheeler, Carlton Books 2000

Living with Zen by Ou Baholyodhin, Tuttle Publishing 2000

Our World in Colour – Vietnam, text by Stephen Bull and photography by Sarah Lock, Asia Books, 1993

South-East Asia Library of Nations by the Editors of Time-Life Books with photographs by Michael Freeman, Time-Life Books, 1987

Thailand A Traveller's Companion, Archipelago Guides, Third Edition 2004

The Arts of Thailand by Steve Van Beek and Luca Invernizzi Tettoni, Periplus 1999

The Book of Batik by Fiona Kerlogue, Archipelago Press, 2004

Thai Buddhas by Dawn F. Rooney, River Books Co., Ltd, 2003

Traditional Indian Textiles by John Gillow and Nicholas Barnard. Thames and Hudson, 1991.

Wabi Sabi Style by James and Sandra Crowley, Gibbs Smith Publisher 2001

This is THE PHILIPPINES by Nigel Hicks, New Holland Publishers Ltd. 2001